JSP: Practical Guide for Java Programmers

JSP | Practical Guide for Java Programmers

Robert J. Brunner

ELSEVIER

AMSTERDAM • BOSTON • HEIDELBERG • LONDON
NEW YORK • OXFORD • PARIS • SAN DIEGO
SAN FRANCISCO • SINGAPORE • SYDNEY • TOKYO
Morgan Kaufmann is an imprint of Elsevier

Senior Editor	Rick Adams
Publishing Services Manager	Simon Crump
Senior Production Editor	Brandy Palacios
Development Editor	Karyn Johnson
Project Management	Graphic World Publishing Services
Technical Illustration	Graphic World Illustration Studio
Composition	Cepha Imaging PVT LTD.
Copyeditor	Graphic World Publishing Services
Proofreader	Graphic World Publishing Services
Indexer	Graphic World Publishing Services
Interior Printer	Maple Press

Designations used by companies to distinguish their products are often claimed as trademarks or registered trademarks. In all instances in which Morgan Kaufmann Publishers is aware of a claim, the product names appear in initial capital or all capital letters. Readers, however, should contact the appropriate companies for more complete information regarding trademarks and registration.

Morgan Kaufmann Publishers
An imprint of Elsevier
340 Pine Street, Sixth Floor
San Francisco, CA 94104-3205
www.mkp.com

07 06 05 04 03   5 4 3 2 1

ISBN: 1-55860-836-2

This book is printed on acid-free paper.

To Eenie, Meenie, Minie, & Moe.

And the One who started it all.

Contents

Preface

It has been more than 10 years since the introduction of the Mosaic Web browser from NCSA when the Web first achieved widespread notice. Early Web pages were generally simple, as people slowly learned the new Hypertext Markup Language (HTML) concepts. As the Internet-browser wars heated up, more people entered the fray, and different technologies, including Java, appeared to assist in the creation of dynamic Web sites. These dynamic sites are what we are accustomed to visiting on the current Web. Of these new technologies, several dominant candidates emerged, including ASP, CGI, and later PHP.

With all these existing technologies, one might wonder why even bother with JavaServer Pages (JSPs)? Although there are many reasons, the answer can be summarized by noting that no other competing technology offers a simple and intuitive interface that supports the full power and portability of the Java programming language.

With the introduction of the JSP 2.0 specification, which is covered in this book, writing JSP pages has become considerably easier, which will soon be reflected in the variety of development tools available. As a result, the number of potential JSP developers will soon increase, as will the corresponding number of JSP Web applications. In summary, now is a great time to learn JavaServer Pages.

Intended Audience

This book has two primary audiences. The first group is professional Web developers who wish to learn how to use JSP technology to build more powerful Web applications. Although little or no knowledge of Java is required to start developing with JSP, such knowledge does not hurt. However, this book does not provide any background on Java. Those who wish to learn more about Java, or any of the other technologies discussed in this book, should look to the resources presented in Appendix B.

The second intended audience group is students in upper-level undergraduate or continuing-education courses in Web application development with Java. This text can be used alone or as a supplement to another text that might provide more details or additional example material. The material in this book requires a Java Virtual Machine (JVM) and a Web-application server, such as the Apache Tomcat server (available for free), that supports the JSP 2.0 specification. The material and example code will work on hardware and operating systems that have these two components.

Approach

Over the last few years, the JSP specification has been rapidly evolving to meet the needs of the Java developer community. As a result, many new features have recently become available, such as an Expression Language (EL), the Java Standard Tag Library (JSTL), and Tag Files. These new concepts can both work with and replace existing techniques. As a future JSP developer, you should be exposed to both the old and new approaches so you can create new applications as well as maintain existing ones. Thus, this text first introduces the original model of using Java code directly within a JSP page. Then, later chapters slowly introduce the newer technologies that allow you to create Java-free JSP pages, which are easier to write and maintain.

The first chapter lays the foundation for the rest of the book. Primarily, this foundation involves Web applications and the related concepts of Hypertext Transport Protocol (HTTP) and Java Servlets. Chapter 1 ends with a brief discussion of the Web application used to demonstrate JSP development throughout this book. As a result, the first chapter can be quickly skimmed by anyone who already has a solid grasp of the basics.

Acknowledgements

The compact nature of this book belies the amount of work required to put it into your hands. Numerous people helped with the entire process, from the original proposal to the completed manuscript.

First, a great deal of thanks goes to the many reviewers, some of whom remained anonymous, whose comments greatly improved the quality of the material presented in this book. A special note of thanks goes to Paul Turcotte, Jon Brisbin, and Jeff Donahoo for their helpful comments. Any errors that remain are entirely my responsibility. If you find any, please let me know. I will maintain an errata page at the book's Web site: *http://www.mkp.com/practical/jsp.*

The people at Morgan Kaufmann, now part of Elsevier, have been enormously helpful. Karyn Johnson, my editor, has been very understanding and supportive, and she is probably even happier than I am to see this book completed. In addition, I would like to thank Rick Adams for his initial support of this project.

Finally, none of this would have been possible without support and love from my family. Now I can finally go out and play.

Feedback

Writing a book is a long and difficult task, aided greatly by having hard deadlines. Despite my best efforts, it is only natural that improvements can be made; otherwise, the book would never get finished. Please feel free to comment on any aspect of this book, via direct email to rb@ncsa.uiuc.edu, or via the book's Web page at *http://www.mkp.com/practical/jsp.*

chapter 1

Introduction to JavaServer Pages

JavaServer Pages (JSP) is a Java technology that allows a developer to rapidly create dynamic Web applications. While other technologies exist, only JSP provides a powerful, portable, and easily extensible framework that supports the development of dynamic Web applications. The JSP specification, or standard, continues to evolve. The latest version, covered in this book, is the JSP 2.0 specification, which introduces new functionality that simplifies the task of JSP page authors—making JSP technology an even better choice for building your next Web application.

This chapter lays the foundation for the rest of the book, by introducing Web applications and the related concepts of Hypertext Transport Protocol (HTTP) and Java Servlets. This chapter ends with a brief discussion of the Web application used to demonstrate JSP development throughout this book.

1.1 Introduction to Web Applications

While JSP technology can be used to build simple Web sites, its real power lies in its ability to provide the foundation for building Web applications. JavaServer Pages can be used to build online banking Web sites, e-commerce sites, public forums, or just about any other type of interactive Web site in which you might be interested.

While other technologies can also play a role in building these types of Web sites and will be discussed in more detail in Chapter 7, JSP has quickly evolved into a powerful technology that can support the construction of dynamic Web applications, even when users have little previous experience. Recent advances like the Expression Language (EL), which is discussed in Chapter 4, and the JSP Standard Tag Library, introduced in Chapter 5,

1

allow small JSP documents that provide powerful capabilities to be created. The JSP spec-ification also allows a developer to construct custom actions, which allow a single line in a JSP page to provide considerable behind-the-scenes functionality. Custom actions are detailed in Chapter 6, where JSP tag files are extensively covered.

At the heart of a JSP Web application, however, are several simple concepts that must be addressed before plunging directly into JavaServer Pages. First, JSP Web applica-tions rely on HTTP to provide client-server communication over the Internet. Second, the JavaServer Page specification is dependent on the Java Servlet specification. As a result, a basic understanding of Java Servlets, including the Servlet lifecycle, is necessary before jumping into building JSP pages. Third, JSP applications follow a simple directory lay-out that groups both configuration information and resources for easier identification and processing. Finally, a Web application requires a *deployment descriptor* that pro-vides configuration information to the Web application server regarding a particular Web application.

1.1.1   The HTTP Model

A JSP-based Web application uses a client-server model, as demonstrated in Figure 1.1. A client makes a request to the server, which responds accordingly. The language that Web servers and Web browsers use to communicate is called HTTP. Currently, HTTP version 1.1 is the standard in use, which defines the commands HEAD, GET, PUT, POST, DELETE, TRACE, OPTIONS, and CONNECT.[1] For a Web-application developer, only GET and POST are generally of interest, as they are the commands used by a client to make a request of a server.

A Uniform Resource Locator (URL) identifies a resource and is the target of a client request. An HTTP message consists of a header that contains information that describes the client to the server, including browser type, possible authentication credentials, the actual HTTP command, and a body that contains the entire content of the message being transmitted.

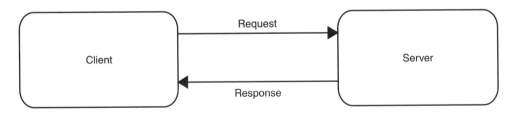

Figure 1.1: The HTTP model.

---

[1] The HTTP/1.1 specification is available at *http://www.w3.org/Protocols/rfc2616/rfc2616.html.*

HTTP is a stateless protocol in which a client makes a request for a resource, and a server responds by providing the resource or an error condition. The server treats subsequent client requests as completely independent requests. Thus, no information, or state, is carried over between subsequent requests from the same client. To support stateful communication, which is mandatory for e-commerce to work, extra information must be transmitted between the client and server to coordinate different HTTP requests into a coherent client request and to allow the server to keep track of a client's actions (such as filling a shopping cart or transferring funds). The process of associating multiple requests together results in a client session.

The server generally manages sessions either by returning data to the client, which will be attached to future requests, or else by adding an additional attribute to an HTTP header. The extra data communicated via the first technique is commonly called a *cookie*. The client can use the cookie as a session identification, or ID, in subsequent requests to identify itself to the server, as shown in Figure 1.2. The second technique is more commonly known as *URL rewriting*, as the session identification is actually appended to the resource URL. This approach proves useful when a cookie cannot be used, which can happen if the client's browser has disabled cookies.

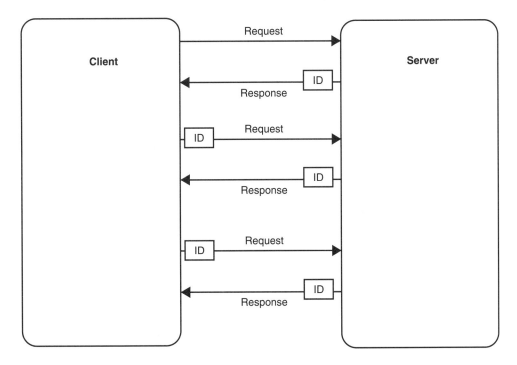

Figure 1.2: Using a cookie named ID to implement a session.

1.1.2   A Brief Introduction to Servlets

The original method for building Web applications using Java was provided by Java Servlets. A Servlet is a Java class that extended the functionality of a server, such as the Apache Web server, to dynamically process incoming requests and generate appropriate responses. Servlets provided a great deal of functionality, allowing early Web sites to leverage the full power of the Java programming language.

This power, however, required anyone who wanted to use Servlets to have a detailed understanding of the Java programming language—something many early Web developers lacked. In response to this difficulty, JSP technology was developed. JSP still provides the full power of the Java programming language, but in a much easier package. JSP technology is layered over the Servlet technology because a JSP page must be translated into a Servlet before the Web server can process it. Thus, a primer on Servlets is useful in understanding how to develop JSP Web applications.

The component of a Web-application server that provides access to JSP resources is called a *container*. This container first translates the JSP page into a Java source code file that by default implements the `javax.servlet.http.HttpServlet` class (experts can change the implementation class, but for the majority of cases, the default works just fine). Next, this Servlet class is compiled into a Java class file, which can be used to process the original client request. Because JSP pages are handled as Servlets, they follow the Servlet lifecycle. In addition, they can use functionality provided by the container in accordance with the Servlet specification, such as Filters and Servlet Listeners. The Servlet application programming interface (API) also includes classes that encapsulate HTTP concepts, such as a request and a response, as well as session information, cookies, and HTTP headers and attributes. Objects that implement these classes are made available to the JSP developer, which simplifies the process of writing Web applications considerably.

The Servlet lifecycle is straightforward (see Figure 1.3) and is managed by the Servlet container. When a request for a Servlet-backed resource is made, the Servlet container locates the implementation class and loads it into a Java Virtual Machine (JVM). For a JSP, the extra steps of translating and compiling the JSP implementation page occur at this stage. After the Servlet class is loaded into the JVM, an object of the Servlet class is instantiated.

The newly instantiated object is ready for the first stage of a Servlet's lifecycle, which is called *initialization*. Any processing that should occur during this stage is placed inside the Servlet's `init` method. This stage is often used to obtain current runtime parameters, read ancillary files, or establish a database connection. Once the initialization stage is complete, the Servlet enters the second stage, called the *service* stage. Processing that occurs during this stage is placed in the `service` method for a `GenericServlet` or in the appropriate HTTP service method, such as `doGet` or `doPost`, for an `HttpServlet`. Once the Servlet is no longer needed, which can occur when the server is being shutdown or resources are being reclaimed, the *destruction* phase is entered. All processing that must occur to clean up a Servlet at this stage is placed in the `destroy` method. This method can be used to close external resources such as database connections or files.

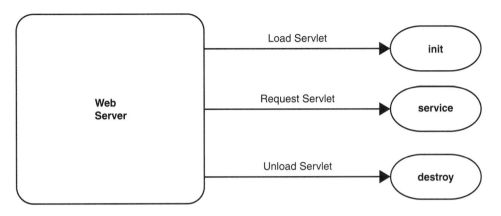

Figure 1.3: The Servlet lifecycle.

A Servlet, and thus a JSP as well, can use one of two approaches to handle multiple, simultaneous client requests for the same resource. These two approaches are demonstrated in Figure 1.4. The first model is the single-threaded model, in which the Web server must create a new instance of the Servlet class for each new client request. This approach simplifies the task of the page developer, but it can adversely affect performance. The second approach is the multithreaded model, in which a single instance of a Servlet class can process multiple requests concurrently. This model generally results in better performance, but it places a burden on the application developer, who must be careful to properly synchronize all shared resources. The details of multithreaded programming and resource synchronization are beyond the scope of this text.[2]

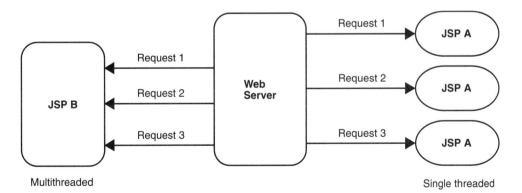

Figure 1.4: A comparison of the two threading models used by Servlets.

---

[2]See *http://java.sun.com/docs/books/tutorial/essential/threads/* for a simple tutorial.

1.1.3 Packaging

Because a Web application may consist of a number of different resources, the JSP and Servlet specifications provide some guidance as to how a Web application should be packaged. First, a Web application is contained in a single directory structure, which is referred to as the *context*. This directory (and all of its contents, including any subdirectories) can be gathered together into a single Web Archive (WAR) file that can be easily deployed.

For example, a Web application could be stored in the pjbank directory, which means that pjbank is the *context*. For the Apache Tomcat server, this directory is, by default, located in the webapps subdirectory of the Tomcat installation directory (for example, C:\tomcat). Thus, the pjbank Web application would be stored in the webapps\pjbank directory and accessed by *http://server:port/pjbank/*, where server is the name of the machine running the application server and port is the port number that the server is listening to for client requests. For most of the examples in this book, this URL translates to *http://localhost:8080/*. Other application servers have different deployment procedures and directory structures; check your server's documentation for the exact details.

JSP pages are generally stored in the root directory of the Web application, which in our example translates to the pjbank directory. This directory can contain other directories, which can contain additional JSP pages, images, JavaScript, or Cascading Style Sheet files. If a subdirectory contains a JSP page, that directory name becomes part of the URL that references the JSP page. Continuing with our example, if we have a subdirectory called loans that contains a JSP page called application.jsp, it can be accessed by a client at *http://server:port/pjbank/loans/application.jsp*. This default behavior can be overridden using the Web application's deployment descriptor, which is described in the next section.

The Servlet specification does define one special directory, called WEB-INF, for web information. This directory contains the deployment descriptor (described in the next section), as well as two other specified directories, called lib and classes. The lib directory is used to store Java archive (JAR) files that are required by the Web application. The classes directory contains the Java classes that implement Servlets, JavaBeans, or Custom Actions, using their fully qualified name. For example, if the pjbank Web application uses a JavaBean called LoginBean that is in the com.pjbank package, it would be stored in the WEB-INF\classes\com\pjbank directory. This concept is displayed in Figure 1.5, which details the Web-application directory structure for the Web application used in Chapter 5.

1.1.4 The Deployment Descriptor

The deployment descriptor for a Web application is used to convey configuration information from the application developer to the Web container that will expose the Web application to clients. The deployment descriptor uses XML Schema Definition (XSD) to encode this information in an XML document. This XML document is named web.xml, and it resides in the WEB-INF subdirectory of the Web application. The root element of this XML document is <web-app>, which specifies the required namespace information as defined

Figure 1.5: The directory structure for the pjbank Web application, to be presented in Chapter 5.

in the Servlet specification. This element forms the core part of the document prolog, or beginning, of the Web-application deployment descriptor.

```
<?xml version="1.0" encoding="ISO-8859-1"?>
<web-app xmlns="http://java.sun.com/xml/ns/j2ee"
 xmlns:xsi="http://www.w3.org/2001/XMLSchema-instance"
 xsi:schemaLocation="http://java.sun.com/xml/ns/j2ee web-app_2_4.xsd"
 version="2.4">

...

[/web-app]
```

Currently, the Web application schema is defined in three different files: one for version 2.4 of the Servlet specification, one for version 2.0 of the JSP Specification, and one for version 1.4 of the Java Enterprise Edition (J2EE) specification. The JSP and J2EE specification schema definition files are included within the Web application schema definition file. Different deployment descriptors are demonstrated throughout this book, providing simple demonstrations of how a web.xml file should look.

The configuration information contained in the deployment descriptor is used to provide mapping between names and implementation classes for Servlets, JSP pages, and Tag Library Descriptors (TLDs). Other types of information contained in the deployment descriptor include security information (technically only required for a J2EE-compliant container), error page handling, MIME-type mappings, and welcome file lists. A partial listing of top-level elements, which can contain their own child elements, is provided in Table 1.1.

1.2   Getting Started with JavaServer Pages

With the preliminaries out of the way, we can now begin to work with JSP technology to develop dynamic Web applications. The rest of this chapter focuses on building a simple

Element Name	Description
context-param	Defines parameters for the current Web application.
display-name	Provides a descriptive name for a Web application.
error-page	Maps an application-specific Web page to an HTTP error code.
filter	Maps a filter name to an implementation class and defines initialization parameters.
jsp-config	Defines configuration information for a group of JSP pages.
login-config	Configures the authentication mechanism used for the current Web application.
mime-mapping	Provides explicit mapping between a file extension and a MIME-type.
servlet	Associates a Servlet name with an implementation class or a JSP file and defines information, such as Servlet initialization parameters.
servlet-mapping	Maps a Servlet name to a Uniform Resource Indicator (URI).
session-config	Defines session-specific information, such as timeout periods.
taglib	Maps a taglib URI to a TLD file.
welcome-file-list	Defines an ordered list of files that can be served for a blank resource request.

Table 1.1: Top-level elements in a Web-application deployment descriptor.

JSP page, and it introduces the Web application that will be featured throughout the rest of the book.

1.2.1   Building a Simple JSP Page

All the examples in this book were tested with version 5.0 of the Tomcat Servlet container. Instructions for obtaining and installing this container are available in Appendix A. Once this container is installed and running, building and testing JSP pages is rather simple (see Figure 1.6). A JSP container must be able to dynamically process a JSP page without needing to be restarted. Thus, JSP pages can be dynamically developed and tested with minimal effort.

The first JSP page shown in this book is welcome.jsp, which is listed following this paragraph. At first glance, you are not expected to understand everything; after all, this is only the start of the book. However, some things should be clear. For example, this JSP page contains Hypertext Markup Language (HTML) elements such as <table> and <tr>, as well as other items that look like elements, such as <jsp:include> and <jsp:param>. This page also contains regular text, such as "Welcome to PJ Bank," which is known as

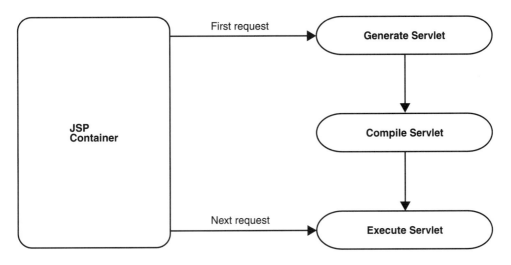

Figure 1.6: The JSP lifecycle.

template text and is passed by the JSP container directly to the client untouched. This page also contains JSP directives, which are identified by the character sequence <%@ and are basically instructions from the JSP developer to the JSP container.

Example 1.1 welcome.jsp

```
<%@ page contentType="text/html" errorPage="exception.jsp"%>
<jsp:include page="header.jsp">
 <jsp:param name="page-title" value="Welcome to PJ Bank"/>
</jsp:include>

<table width="100%">
 <tr>
  <td valign="top" width="25%"> <jsp:include page="left-banner.jsp" /></td>
  <td valign="top">
   Welcome to PJ Bank, the persistent bank for those who like Java!
  </td>
  <td valign="top" width="25%"> <%@ include file="right-banner.jspf" %></td>
 </tr>
</table>
<jsp:include page="footer.jsp"/>
```

All the different constructs used in JSP pages will be explained in the rest of the book. Sometimes, however, it can be useful to look at the Servlet implementation class generated by the container for a JSP page. For version 5.0 of the Tomcat server, if the original

JSP page is located in the webapps\pjbank-1 directory, the implementation Servlet class will be created and compiled in the work\Catalina\localhost\pjbank-1 subdirectory of the Tomcat installation. The implementation class for welcome.jsp is partially shown as follows in welcome_jsp.java (the whole file would occupy several pages).

Example 1.2 welcome_jsp.java

```java
package org.apache.jsp;

import javax.servlet.*;
import javax.servlet.http.*;
import javax.servlet.jsp.*;

public final class welcome_jsp extends org.apache.jasper.runtime.HttpJspBase
  implements org.apache.jasper.runtime.JspSourceDependent {
...
 public void _jspService(HttpServletRequest request, HttpServletResponse response)
    throws java.io.IOException, ServletException {

 JspFactory _jspxFactory = null;
 PageContext pageContext = null;
 HttpSession session = null;
 ServletContext application = null;
 ServletConfig config = null;
 JspWriter out = null;
 Object page = this;
 JspWriter _jspx_out = null;

 try {
  _jspxFactory = JspFactory.getDefaultFactory();
  response.setContentType("text/html");
  pageContext = _jspxFactory.getPageContext(this, request, response,
                "exception.jsp", true, 8192, true);
  application = pageContext.getServletContext();
  config = pageContext.getServletConfig();
  session = pageContext.getSession();
  out = pageContext.getOut();
  _jspx_out = out;

  out.write("\n");
  org.apache.jasper.runtime.JspRuntimeLibrary.include(request, response,
   "header.jsp" + (("header.jsp").indexOf('?')>0? '&': '?') +
    org.apache.jasper.runtime.JspRuntimeLibrary.URLEncode("page-title",
    request.getCharacterEncoding())+ "=" +
     org.apache.jasper.runtime.JspRuntimeLibrary.URLEncode(
      "Welcome to PJ Bank", request.getCharacterEncoding()), out, false);
```

```
  out.write("\n\n");
  out.write("<table width=\"100%\">\n ");
  out.write("<tr>\n ");
  out.write("<td valign=\"top\" width=\"25%\"> ");
  org.apache.jasper.runtime.JspRuntimeLibrary.include(request, response,
   "left-banner.jsp", out, false);
  out.write(" ");
  out.write("</td>\n ");
...
  out.write("</tr>\n");
  out.write("</table>\n");
  out.write(" ");
  out.write("</td>\n ");
  out.write("</tr>\n");
  out.write("</table>\n");
...
 }
 }
}
```

This implementation class can be very instructive, and it is sometimes the best way to debug a Web application. In this case, the translated JSP page is turned into a Servlet called welcome_jsp. The service method for this class is called _jspService, which takes an HTTP request and a response object as input parameters. The first thing this method does is initialize the JSP-implicit objects a JSP developer can use. After this, the template text is written to the Servlet's output stream, and various external resources are included in the current output stream.

This implementation class also demonstrates one of the primary advantages of JSP technology over its Servlet underpinnings. Notice how out.write method calls dominate the Servlet, while the JSP page just explicitly contains the template text. This shows how easy it is to write JSP applications quickly, as HTML elements and regular text can be placed directly into the JSP page. In fact, an HTML page can be converted into a JSP page by changing the file's extension from *.html* to *.jsp* and placing it within a Web application.

1.2.2   The PJ Bank Web Application

The JSP page shown in the last section is actually part of the Web application that is constructed throughout this text. This Web application is an online banking Web site for a fictitious bank, called PJ Bank, which is short for Persistent Java Bank. Most of the book focuses on the initial welcome page and shows how different concepts change the way the welcome page can be built. Other areas that are discussed include a login page and an accounts page controlled by an XML file and, later, a database connection.

In addition to this explicit Web application, the exercises at the end of each chapter guide readers in the construction of an online shopping site. Remember that regardless of the Web application type, it is important to test a Web application using as many different Web browsers as possible. Clients who cannot work with a Web application will not be your clients for long.

Exercises

1. Using the HTTP/1.1 specification, identify five different HTTP Headers.

2. Describe the HTTP communication model in your own words.

3. Describe the Servlet lifecycle in your own words.

4. Download and install the Apache Jakarta Tomcat server software. Also install the book's sample code. Instructions are provided in Appendix A.

5. Outline the necessary components of an online shopping Web application, including the process of shopping, buying, and tracking items.

chapter 2

The Fundamentals of JavaServer Pages

The JavaServer Page specification is continually evolving in an attempt to improve the development process for Web applications built with J2EE. This evolutionary process, however, can leave a conflicting wake of multiple approaches to solving the same task. In this chapter, we will cover the fundamental JSP constructs, which although still applicable, have been overshadowed by more recent developments such as custom actions, expression language, and tag files, all of which are discussed in later chapters.

Thus, even though there are alternative approaches that may be more appropriate or even offer a better solution, a solid understanding of the JSP basics is important. As an example, the original JSP development approach outlined in this chapter, formally termed *page-centric*, can often be useful for rapid prototyping. Or, you may need to work with an existing JSP application that relies on a page-centric approach to JSP application development. Finally, understanding limitations of this original approach demonstrates the power of the more recent additions to the JSP specification.

2.1 Directives

JSP directives are instructions to the JSP container that are processed during the page translation process. Although there are six directives defined in the JSP 2.0 specification, only three are valid within a JSP page.[1] These three are the page, include, and taglib directives.

---

[1] See sections 1.10 and 8.5 of the JSP specification, which can be found at *http://java.sun.com/products/jsp*, for more detail.

13

The other three directives, tag, attribute, and variable, are valid only within JSP Tag Files and are discussed in Chapter 6.

Directives are indicated in a JSP page using the directive start tag, followed by the directive name, any directive attributes, and terminated by the directive end tag, as shown in the following example:

```
<%@ page info="The page directive" %>
```

Optional white space is allowed between start and end tags and is ignored during the processing of the directive. While JSP directives do not directly produce any output into the current output stream, any new lines within the directive will be added to the template text of the JSP page. The alternative XML syntax for each directive is presented below in the appropriate subsections.

2.1.1   The Page Directive

The page directive is used to communicate information about a specific JSP page to the JSP container. This information is used to generate the underlying Servlet and includes, among other things, the programming language used within the JSP page; the classes that need to be imported; the class, if any, extended by the current JSP; and the threading behavior of the current JSP page. The 14 attributes for the page directive are listed in Table 2.1 and are detailed in the rest of this section.

The language attribute specifies the scripting language used in the JSP page. Currently, the only legal (and thus the default) value for this attribute is java. However, future versions of the JSP specification may define new values.

The import attribute specifies all the types provided to the current JSP page by the JSP container. These types must be either fully qualified class names or package names followed by the asterisk character (*). This attribute is the only one that can appear multiple times within the same translation unit without forcing an error condition. Multiple import attributes are cumulative. This attribute is currently defined only if the language attribute is set to java.

```
<%@ page language="java" imports="java.util.*" %>
```

The extends attribute specifies the fully qualified class name of the superclass to be used for the generated Servlet class that provides the functionality of the current JSP page. Because the Java programming language permits only single inheritance, this attribute is rarely used as it forces the developer to provide all the necessary Hypertext Transport Protocol (HTTP) functionality normally provided automatically by the JSP container (via the HttpServlet class).

```
<%@ page extends="com.persistentJava.BaseJSP" %>
```

The session attribute is a Boolean attribute that specifies whether the current JSP page is participating in an HTTP session. The default value is true, meaning that an implicit scripting variable named session is available within the current JSP page. If the attribute

Attribute Name	Description
language	Indicates the scripting language used within JSP page.
import	Lists Java classes to import into the generated Servlet.
extends	Used to indicate a superclass for the generated Servlet.
session	Indicates if JSP page is participating in a session.
buffer	Indicates the size of the buffer for the current JSP.
autoflush	Indicates whether the buffer is automatically written when it is full.
isThreadSafe	Indicates if the JSP can handle multiple requests at the same time.
isErrorPage	Indicates if the JSP page is designed to handle error conditions.
errorPage	Specifies a JSP that will handle error conditions.
info	Descriptive comment for the current JSP.
contentType	Specifies the MIME type and character encoding for response.
pageEncoding	Specifies the character encoding for the current JSP page.
isScriptingEnabled	Controls whether JSP scripting elements are allowed in current JSP.
isELEnabled	Controls whether JSP EL expressions are allowed in current JSP.

Table 2.1: The 14 attributes for the page directive.

is set to false, this implicit scripting variable is not available, and any attempt to reference it will result in a fatal translation error.

```
<%@ page session="true" %>
```

The buffer attribute controls the buffering behavior of the current output stream. The default value for this attribute is 8kb, for 8 kilobytes. Allowed values for this attribute are none for no buffering, in which case output is sent directly to the client, or a numerical value that indicates the minimum buffer size in kilobytes. If a size is provided, the suffix kb is mandatory.

The autoflush attribute is a Boolean attribute that controls whether the underlying buffer, assuming the buffer attribute is not set to none, is automatically written whenever the buffer becomes full or an exception is raised. The default value of this attribute is true, meaning that by default a JSP translation unit will write into an 8-kb buffer that is flushed whenever it becomes full.

```
<%@ page buffer="8kb" autoflush="true" %>
```

The isThreadSafe attribute is a Boolean attribute that specifies whether the JSP page can handle multiple concurrent requests. If set to false, the JSP container must sequentially process requests in the order they are received. If set to true, the JSP container can process multiple requests simultaneously. If set to true, which is the default value, all shared resource access must be properly synchronized.

```
<%@ page isThreadSafe="true" %>
```

The isErrorPage attribute is a Boolean attribute that indicates whether the current JSP page is designed to handle error conditions from other JSP pages. If this attribute is set to true, the implicit exception object is made available by the JSP container to the JSP page. This exception object provides access to the original exception condition. The default value is false.

The errorPage attribute defines a Uniform Resource Locator (URL), typically another JSP page, to be used to handle any error conditions thrown but not caught during the execution of the current JSP page.

```
<%@ page isErrorPage="false" errorPage="error.jsp" %>
```

The info attribute is a string that provides a descriptive comment concerning the JSP page. This string is accessible via the generated Servlet's getServletInfo method.

```
<%@ page info="Hello World JSP page" %>
```

The contentType attribute is a string that specifies the character encoding and the MIME type for the current JSP page's response. This attribute can specify the MIME type and the character encoding directly using the charset=CHARSET substring. The default value for the MIME type is text/html, and the default value for the character encoding is ISO-8859-1, or UTF-8 if the JSP page is written in XML syntax. Any specified character encoding must be a legally defined character set to become valid.[2]

```
<%@ page contentType="text/html;charset=ISO-8859-1" %>
```

The pageEncoding attribute specifies the character encoding used in the current JSP page. By default, the character encoding specified in the contentType attribute is used. The value use in a pageEncoding attribute must be a legally defined character set.

The isScriptingEnabled attribute is a Boolean attribute that specifies whether JSP scripting elements, such as declarations, expressions, and scriptlets (all defined later in this chapter), are allowed within the current JSP page. The default value is true, but if it is set to false, any attempt to use a scripting element will result in a translation error.

The isELEnabled attribute is a Boolean attribute that specifies whether Expression Language (EL) expressions (defined in Chapter 4) are evaluated within the current JSP page. The default value is true. If set to false, any EL expression is ignored within the current JSP page.

```
<%@ page isScriptingEnabled="true" isELEnabled="true" %>
```

The XML syntax for the JSP page directive is similar in appearance to the standard syntax. However, the jsp.directive.page start tag is used, and the element contains only

---

[2]See the IANA Web site for complete details *(http://www.iana.org/assignments/character-sets)*.

attributes; it is therefore empty. The following example is identical in functionality to the first page directive shown earlier.

```
<jsp:directive.page language="java" imports="java.util.* " />
```

2.1.2 The Include Directive

The include directive is used to specify static resources that should be included within the current JSP page translation unit. Thus, you can use the JSP include directive to include a standard page header, style sheets, or client-side scripts. The include directive has a single attribute, called file, that specifies the URL for the resource that should be included. The following example demonstrates using the include directive to include a standard JSP header page in the current translation unit.

```
<%@ include file="header.jsp" %>
```

The include directive has a similar XML syntax to the page directive, as shown in the following example.

```
<jsp:directive.include file="header.jsp" />
```

2.1.3 The Taglib Directive

Later in this chapter we will cover the JSP standard actions, which encapsulate functionality using an XML tag-like syntax. A recent introduction to JSP development is the ability to create custom actions, or custom tags, that are grouped into a tag library. The taglib directive is used to define a prefix and location about a tag library to the current JSP page. Custom actions are covered in detail in Chapter 6. The taglib directive has three attributes.

The prefix attribute is used to define the namespace prefix that will signify a custom action in the current JSP page. Certain character sequences are reserved,[3] and empty prefixes are not allowed.

The uri attribute specifies either an absolute or relative Uniform Resource Indicator (URI) that uniquely identifies the tag library descriptor specified with the current taglib directive.

```
<%@ taglib uri="http://www.persistentjava.com/tags/pjbank" prefix="pjbank" %>
```

The tagdir attribute can be used in lieu of the uri attribute to specify the local directory that contains the tag library descriptor specified with the current taglib directive. The tagdir attribute must start with /WEB-INF/tags and must point to a directory that exists or else a translation error will be generated.

```
<%@ taglib tagdir="/WEB-INF/tags/pjbank" prefix="pjbank" %>
```

---

[3] See section 1.10.2 of the JSP specification for a complete list.

The XML syntax for the `tagdir` directive is unique relative to the other two directives because the tag directory is specified by an attribute of the `jsp.root` element. The following example demonstrates the `tagdir` directive using XML syntax, with the same result as the first `tagdir` directive example above.

```
<jsp:root ...
 xmlns:pjbank="http://www.persistentjava.com/tags/pjbank">
...
</jsp:root>
```

2.2 JSP Declarations

Following the page directive and any introductory HTML elements, the next item is the JSP declaration element. A declaration element produces no output into the JSP response; instead, it is used to declare globally visible variables and methods within a JSP page. A declaration element is enclosed within a <%! start tag and a %> end tag. When using the XML syntax, these change to `<jsp:declaration>` and `</jsp:declaration>`. In addition, a semicolon must terminate all statements within a JSP declaration.

Because these declarations have global scope, they should be used with care. For example, you probably would not want to acquire any expensive resource, such as a database connection, in a JSP declaration because this can create synchronization nightmares in addition to resource leaks. However, if you have frequently used methods, you can declare them in the declaration section, which will be translated directly into a method within the page-implementation Servlet.

One area where a declaration element can be very useful is in providing explicit implementations for the `init` and/or `destroy` methods for the JSP page. If you recall from Chapter 1, the Servlet lifecycle is the initialization, or init, phase, then the service invocation phase, followed by the destroy phase. A JSP container automatically handles the service phase for the developer. However, the init and destroy phases are not handled. To provide explicit definitions for these phases, you can create `jspInit` and `jspDestroy` methods within the JSP declaration element. The following JSP page demonstrates this capability, in this case writing messages to the console (which, depending on your JSP container, may be redirected to an application log file).

Example 2.1 phases.jsp

```
<%!
public void jspInit() {
 System.out.println("JSP Initialization") ;
}

public void jspDestroy() {
 System.out.println("JSP Destroy") ;
}
```

```
%>
<html>
<body>
<h1> Hello World, Declaration Example </h1>
</body>
</html>
```

2.3 Expressions

The standard JSP expression is just a Java expression that is evaluated at run-time by the JSP container. JSP expression elements are enclosed within the <%= start tag and the %> end tag and are not terminated by a semicolon because they are merely expressions and not statements. In XML syntax, the expression is enclosed within the <jsp:expression> and </jsp:expression> tags.

An expression can consist of a variable name, in which case the result is the value of the variable; a method call, in which case the result is the return value of the method; or any legal combinations of variables, methods, and operators. The following JSP page demonstrates several JSP expressions, as shown in Figure 2.1.

Figure 2.1: The rendered version of expressions.jsp.

Example 2.2 expressions.jsp

```
<%! int global = 0 ; %>
<html>
<body>
<h1> Today is <%= new java.util.Date() %> </h1>
<hr/>
<h2> This page has been accessed <%= global++ %> times.</h2>
</body>
</html>
```

2.4 Scriptlets

Early on, one of the biggest reasons for the adoption of JSP pages was the ability to place fragments of Java code directly in a JSP page. These fragments are known as *scriptlets*, and they simplified Java developers' transition into Web-application developers. A scriptlet can contain any legal Java code and, therefore, must follow the syntactical rules for Java code, including the fact that individual statements must be terminated by a semicolon.

Scriptlets are enclosed within the <% start tag and the %> end tag or, in XML syntax, between the <jsp:scriptlet> start tag and the </jsp:scriptlet> end tag. Unlike the declaration element described earlier, any variables declared within a scriptlet are local to the scriptlet itself. Scriptlets allow HTML and Java code to be freely intermixed, which can be useful for looping over data structures. One caveat, however, is that you must remember to wrap all Java code, including curly braces, with the scriptlet tags. The following example, scriptlet.jsp, demonstrates this, as shown in Figure 2.2, by modifying expressions.jsp to display a local counter as well as specific data. In practice, this data might be obtained dynamically from a database or Web service, but for simplicity, it is hard-coded into the scriptlet.

Example 2.3 scriptlet.jsp

```
<%! int global = 0 ; %>
<html>
<body>
<h1> Today is <%= new java.util.Date() %> </h1>
<hr/>
<h2> This page has been accessed <%= global++ %> times.</h2>
<hr/>
<%
 int local = 0 ;
String[] names = {"Cookie 1", "Cookie 2", "Cookie 3"} ;
String[] values = {"Chocolate Chip", "Peanut Butter", "Sugar"};
```

Today is Wed Apr 02 13:09:51 CST 2003

This page has been accessed 5 times.

Cookie 1 Chocolate Chip
Cookie 2 Peanut Butter
Cookie 3 Sugar

This page has been accessed 0 times.

Figure 2.2: The rendered version of scriptlet.jsp.

```
%>
<table>
 <tr>
<%
 for(int i = 0 ; i < names.length; i ++) {
%>
  <td> <%= names[i] %></td>
  <td> <%= values[i] %> </td>
 </tr>
<% } %>
</table>

<hr/>
```

```
<h2> This page has been accessed <%= local++ %> times. </h2>

</body>
</html>
```

Notice how this example freely combines Java expressions and code with HTML elements, greatly simplifying the creation of the HTML table, as well as adding dynamic content.

The JSP development approach that uses JSP declarations, expressions, and scriptlets within a JSP page is known as the *page-centric model*. This approach has suffered serious criticism due to the complications of careless mixing of HTML elements and Java code. Likewise, the requirement that a Web-application developer know Java to use JSP technology limited the pool of potential programmers. In response to this challenge, the JSP specification has incorporated new technologies, such as custom actions and EL, which separate the responsibilities for page layout and design from the responsibilities of developing dynamic actions. Nevertheless, JSP scriptlets are legal JSP elements and are often useful in prototyping new features, which can be moved into custom actions, JavaBeans, or Servlets once the code is working successfully.

2.5 Comments

Comments in a JSP page come in three different flavors. First are comments that are visible in the generated HTML page, known as *output comments*. These comments follow the rules for HTML comments and are enclosed between <!-- and --> tags. Because output comments are considered template text by the JSP container, they are passed untouched to the client. They can, however, contain additional JSP constructs, such as a JSP expression element, that are processed, resulting in a dynamic comment.

The second type of comment is the *JSP comment*, which is also known as a *hidden comment* because it does not appear in the generated HTML page. JSP comments are enclosed in <%-- and --%> tags. The JSP container strips these comments during the page-translation phase.

The final type of comment is a *scripting comment*, which should be used to comment the code contained in a JSP declaration or scripting element. Scripting comments, because they are used within Java constructs, must follow the rules for using comments as defined by the Java programming language. The following example, comment.jsp, demonstrates all three types of comments.

Example 2.4 comment.jsp

```
<html>
<body>
<!-- This file generated at <%= new java.util.Date() %> -->
```

```
<%!
int global = 0 ; // This is a global counter
%>

<% -- The following JSP elements print out the counter information --%>

</h2>
This page has been accessed <%=global++ %> times
</h2>

</body>
</html>
```

These different components—directives, declarations, expressions, scriptlets, comments, and template text—can be combined in many different ways to form a JSP page. However, a common approach is to place the page directive first, followed by any JSP declarations. After that, scriptlets can be intermixed with include directives and template text, which might have embedded expressions, as shown in Figure 2.3.

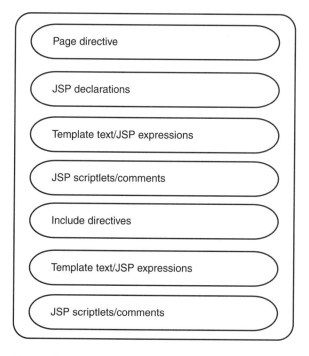

Figure 2.3: A typical usage pattern of different components within a JSP page.

2.6 Scope

A Web application can be complicated with multiple JSP pages, JavaBeans, Tag Files, and Servlets working together within a server to handle numerous client requests. To simplify the development and operation of a Web application, the JSP specification provides a mechanism for limiting the visibility of objects, or variables, to other objects within a JSP Web application. Formally, the visibility of an object is called its *scope*, of which four different levels are defined in the JSP specification. These four levels are detailed in the following list, which presents them in order of increasing visibility.

1. *Page scope* implies that objects are visible only within the JSP page in which they were created. Once a JSP page has completed its service phase for a given client request, which can occur when a page has finished being processed or when a request is forwarded on to another page, any references to objects with page scope are released. This allows the Java Virtual Machine (JVM) to garbage-collect any objects with page scope; thus, any results calculated during the processing of a JSP page are lost and must be recalculated with every new client request.

2. *Request scope* is a step above page scope, in that objects with request scope are visible during the entire processing of a client request. This can involve multiple JSP pages, JavaBeans, Servlets, or Tag Libraries that might collaborate in processing a single request.

3. *Session scope* extends request scope to allow objects to remain visible across multiple requests from the same client. This is important for many real-world JSP Web applications, such as e-commerce, in which a user should not need to continually log into a site or when a user is adding items to a shopping cart.

4. *Application scope* extends session scope to allow objects to be visible across multiple sessions. Essentially, this means an object can be shared across multiple requests from different clients. While some of this functionality is best left to external resources, such as a database, application scope might prove useful when an application wants to maintain an up-to-date inventory or provide controlled resource throttling.

2.7 Implicit Objects

A JSP container provides a JSP page with access to specific implicit objects through scripting variables. In practice, these objects are declared at the start of the Servlet that implements a JSP page. These implicit objects can be accessed in a JSP scriptlet, a JSP expression, or as part of an EL expression. The nine implicit objects are listed in Table 2.2, along with the relevant API class or interface that details the functionality provided. The implicit objects are described in more detail in the sections that follow.

Implict Object	Description	API
request	Provides access to the client's request.	ServletRequest
response	Provides access to the JSP's response.	ServletResponse
session	Shares information across client requests.	HttpSession
exception	Accesses error status.	JspException
application	Accesses application-level objects.	ServletContext
pageContext	Access the JSP object container.	PageContext
out	Access the JSP output stream.	JspWriter
config	Contains configuration information.	ServletConfig
page	Provides a reference to current JSP.	Object

Table 2.2: The nine implicit objects.

2.7.1 The Request Object

The request object implements a protocol-dependent subclass of the javax.servlet. ServletRequest class. In practice, this is generally the HttpServletRequest class,[4] which provides access to HTTP parameters, attributes, headers, and cookies within a JSP page.[5] The following example JSP pages demonstrate common uses of the request object. First, headers.jsp displays all HTTP Headers from a specific request in an HTML table.

Example 2.5 headers.jsp

```
<%@ page import="java.util.* " %>
<html>
<body>
<table>
<%
String header ;
Enumeration headers = request.getHeaderNames();
while(headers.hasMoreElements()) {
 header = (String)headers.nextElement();
%>
<tr>
  <td> <%= header %> </td>
  <td> <%= request.getHeader(header) %> </td>
```

---

[4]The complete API for the HttpServletRequest class is available at *http://java.sun.com/j2ee/1.4/ docs/api/javax/servlet/http/HttpServletRequest.html*.
[5]For more details on the HTTP protocol see *http://www.w3.org/Protocols/rfc2616/rfc2616.html*.

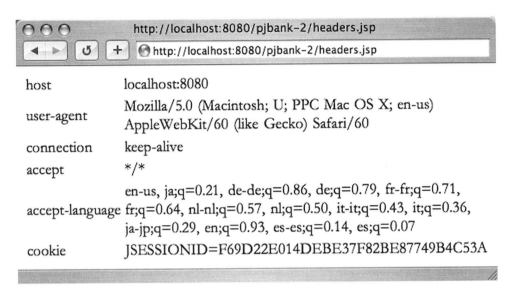

Figure 2.4: Displaying request headers.

```
  </tr>
<% } %>
</table>
</body>
</html>
```

This example is fairly straightforward and produces the Web page shown in Figure 2.4. After importing the java.util package, so that the Enumeration class is available, we iterate through the header enumeration, displaying each HTTP Header with its associated value. A similar idiom is used to access any attributes associated with the session with which a JSP page is associated. In this case, rather than calling the getHeader Names method, you must call the getAttributeNames method to obtain the Enumeration containing all the attributes and the getAttribute method, as opposed to the getHeader method, to obtain the value for each attribute name. All of these methods are accessible from the implicit request object.

One of the most common uses for JSP pages is to process client data. When using the HTTP protocol, this information is communicated in HTTP parameters. In parameters.jsp, we display each HTTP parameter along with its associated values.

Example 2.6 parameters.jsp

```
<%@ page import="java.util.*" %>
<html>
```

```
<body>
<%
String name ;
String[] values ;
Enumeration names = request.getParameterNames();
while(names.hasMoreElements()) {
 name = (String)names.nextElement();
 values = request.getParameterValues(name) ;
%>
 <% = name %> <br/>
 <ul>
<%
 for(int i = 0 ; i < values.length ; i++) {
%>
  <li> <%= values[i] %> </li>
<% } %>
 </ul>
<% } %>
</body>
</html>
```

In this example, we once again use the Enumeration class to process the parameters associated with the specified HTTP request. Because a parameter can have multiple values, we must also loop over all possible values for each parameter, hence the double loop in parameters.jsp. The final result is displayed in Figure 2.5.

2.7.2 The Response Object

The response object is the opposite of the request object and implements a protocol-dependent subclass of the javax.servlet.ServletResponse class. Generally this means the response object implements the HttpServletResponse class.[6] As a result, it allows a JSP page to control the HTTP response returned to the client. This includes setting the response HTTP headers, the HTTP status code, the content type, and even cookies. To demonstrate, cookies.jsp shows how a JSP page can use cookies: first to set them in the response and second to retrieve them from the request.

Example 2.7 cookies.jsp

```
<html>
<body>
```

---

[6]The complete API for the HttpServletResponse class is available at *http://java.sun.com/j2ee/1.4/docs/api/javax/servlet/http/HttpServletResponse.html.*

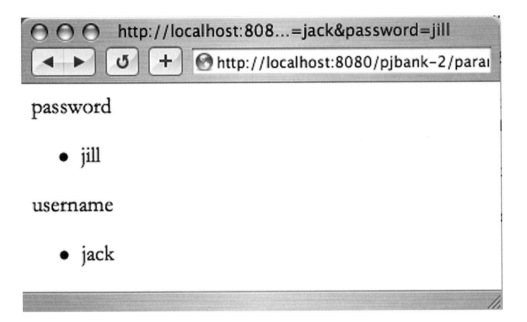

Figure 2.5: Displaying request parameters. Note that this only shows something if the request has parameters.

```
<%
Cookie[] cookies = request.getCookies() ;
if(cookies.length > 1) {
%>
<table>
 <tr>
<%
 for(int i = 0 ; i < cookies.length ; i ++) {
%>
  <td> <%= cookies[i].getName() %> </td>
  <td> <%= cookies[i].getValue() %> </td>
 </tr>
<% } %>
</table>
<%
}else {
 response.addCookie(new Cookie("Cookie 1", "Chocolate Chip")) ;
 response.addCookie(new Cookie("Cookie 2", "Peanut Butter")) ;
 response.addCookie(new Cookie("Cookie 3", "Sugar")) ;
%>
<h2> Cookies Initialized, Reload Page to see them </h2>
<% } %>
```

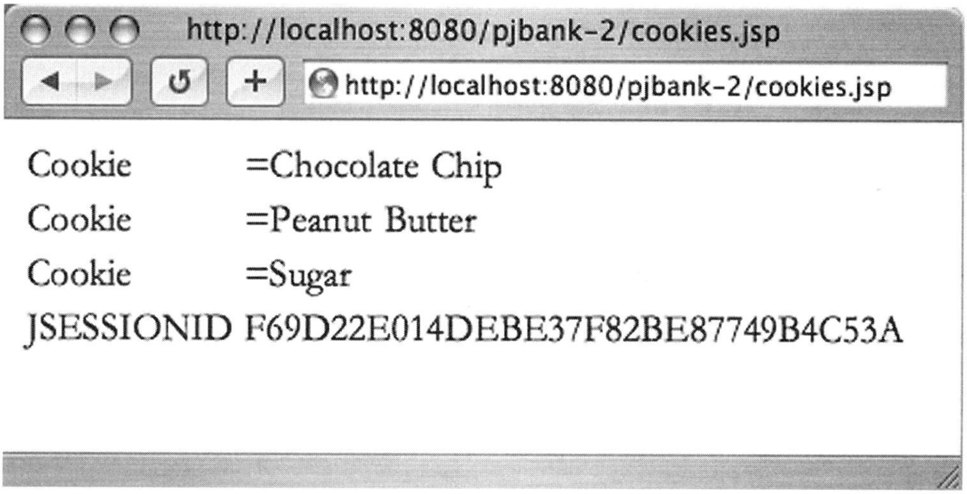

```
Cookie        =Chocolate Chip
Cookie        =Peanut Butter
Cookie        =Sugar
JSESSIONID F69D22E014DEBE37F82BE87749B4C53A
```

Figure 2.6: The rendered version of cookies.jsp after the page has been reloaded.

```
</body>
</html>
```

In this simple example, we first retrieve all cookies from the client request. If there are no cookies (which should be the default when the page is first loaded), we set several cookies and inform the client to reload the page. Once the request contains cookies, we iterate through them all and display them in an HTML table, as shown in Figure 2.6.

Other useful methods associated with the response object include the following:

- setContentType to specify the MIME type of the HTTP response
- setError to set the status code of the HTTP response to a specific HTTP error code
- setStatus to set the status of the HTTP response to a specific HTTP status code
- setHeader to associate a value with an HTTP Header
- addHeader to add a new value to an existing HTTP Header
- setDateHeader to add a date header
- setIntHeader to add an integer value header

2.7.3 The Session Object

Because the HTTP protocol is stateless, an additional mechanism is needed to share information between subsequent client requests. The mechanism for doing this in a Web application is a session object, which is a container-specific class that implements the HttpSession interface.[7] The session object is used to associate a name with an object, allowing subsequent client requests to reference the object using only the name. Sessions are extremely important in developing Web applications, and we will be returning to them throughout this book.

To remember the session identification itself, most JSP containers use a special cookie called the *SessionID* (these details are hidden from the developer). If the client does not allow cookies to be persisted at the client, alternative techniques must be used. These more complicated techniques are beyond the scope of this book. Although it is possible, as demonstrated below, to use the session object directly, it is more likely that you will use it indirectly with either a JavaBean or custom action that uses session-level scope.

To demonstrate the session object, the following JSP page, session.jsp, modifies the cookie.jsp page to use a session object to store the data, rather than several cookies.

Example 2.8 session.jsp

```
<%@ page import="java.util.*" %>
<html>
<body>
<%
Properties cookies = (Properties)session.getAttribute("cookies") ;

String[] names = {"Cookie 1", "Cookie 2", "Cookie 3"} ;
String[] values = {"Chocolate Chip", "Peanut Butter", "Sugar"};

if(cookies != null) {
%>
<table>
 <tr>
<%
 for(int i = 0 ; i < cookies.size(); i ++) {
%>
  <td> <%= names[i] %></td>
  <td> <%= cookies.getProperty(names[i]) %> </td>
 </tr>
<% } %>
</table>
<%
}else {

 cookies = new Properties() ;
 for(int i = 0 ; i < names.length ; i ++)
```

---

[7]The complete API for the HttpSession class is available at *http://java.sun.com/j2ee/1.4/docs/api/ javax/servlet/http/HttpSession.html.*

Cookie 1 Chocolate Chip

Cookie 2 Peanut Butter

Cookie 3 Sugar

Figure 2.7: The rendered version of session.jsp after the page has been reloaded.

```
    cookies.setProperty(names[i], values[i]) ;

  session.setAttribute("cookies", cookies) ;
%>
<h2> Session Initialized, Reload Page to see the result </h2>
<% } %>
</body>
</html>
```

In this example, we first import the java.util package to be able to use the Properties class. We then retrieve the named session. If it is not null, we retrieve the information from the session and display it in a table. Otherwise, we need to populate the session. Notice that we could have associated any object with a given name within the session, which demonstrates the power of sessions. All that is required is to set the session attribute and, when retrieving the session attribute, cast it to the appropriate Java class. The resulting Web page is shown in Figure 2.7.

2.7.4 The Exception Object

To simplify development, JSP pages can ignore error handling and instead use the errorPage attribute of the page directive to indicate a resource that will handle error

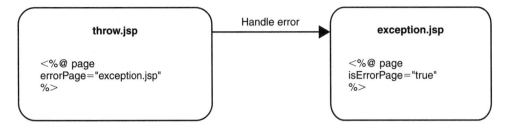

Figure 2.8: The JSP error-handling mechanism.

conditions that might arise during the execution of the current JSP page. The error condition information is encapsulated within the exception object,[8] which is accessible only to JSP pages that are declared as error pages via the page directive's isErrorPage attribute. The JSP error-handling procedure is demonstrated in Figure 2.8.

To demonstrate the use of the exception object, we first need to create a JSP page to handle an error condition. In production environments, you generally want to log all relevant details and possibly email information to the relevant administrator for prompt action. In this example, shown in exception.jsp, however, we merely print out a suitable message (but not the stack dump) associated with the exception.

Example 2.9 exception.jsp

```
<%@ page isErrorPage="true" %>
<html>
<body>
<h2> An error has occurred! </h2>
<% = exception.getMessage() %>
</body>
</html>
```

To demonstrate this error page, we need a JSP page that throws an exception, which is shown in throw.jsp below (the extra if statement is present to make the JSP compiler happy). The end result is shown in Figure 2.9.

Example 2.10 throw.jsp

```
<%@ page errorPage="exception.jsp" %>
<%
if(true)
```

---

[8]This object is a container-specific implementation of the JspException interface, which is available at *http://java.sun.com/j2ee/1.4/docs/api/javax/servlet/jsp/JspException.html*.

Figure 2.9: The demonstration of an exception condition.

```
  throw new Exception("This is a test") ;
%>
```

2.7.5 The Other Implicit Objects

The other five implicit objects are less frequently used directly within a JSP page. These objects are used occasionally when writing Servlets, JavaBeans, or custom actions, however, as they can simplify the sharing of data within a Web application. For more details on any of these implicit objects, see the API documentation for the class or interface listed for each object.[9]

The application object is the most used of the remaining implicit objects; it provides a mechanism for sharing data at the application-level scope. The application object is an instance of a container-specific class that, for the HTTP protocol, implements the javax.servlet.ServletContext interface. As was the case with the session object, a JSP Web application generally does not directly interact with the application object. Instead it is indirectly used by JavaBeans or custom actions, which will be discussed later

---

[9]The root page for all J2EE technologies is *http://java.sun.com/j2ee/1.4/docs/api/index.html*, which contains the Servlet and JSP class and interface specifications.

in this book. One additional use for the application object is to log messages to the container's application log file.

The pageContext implicit object essentially acts as a super-implicit object; it provides direct access to the other implicit objects within a JSP page, as well as access to the different scope levels and page attributes. When using the HTTP protocol, the pageContext object is an instance of a container-provided class that extends the javax. servlet.jsp.PageContext class.

The out implicit object provides access to the output stream used by the JSP page. Because the JSP container automatically writes text into the output stream, this object is almost never used directly by a JSP application. For applications that use the HTTP protocol, the out object is a container-provided implementation class that extends the javax.servlet.jsp.JspWriter class.

The config implicit object is used by the JSP container to pass configuration information to the JSP during initialization, and it includes information defined in the Web-application deployment descriptor (more commonly known as web.xml). As a result, a Web application developer rarely uses the config object.

The page implicit object is assigned to a container-provided class that extends the Java Object class. The page object provides a reference to the current JSP page, and thus, it can be loosely translated as the this object within a JSP page. There are almost no reasons for a developer to directly use the page object.

2.8   Standard Actions

Standard actions are predefined JSP elements that implement specific functionality. As is the case with all actions (or tags), they follow the rules for XML, and thus, they do not have alternative syntactical representations. With each new JSP specification, the list of standard actions increases, as do the actions' complexity. Currently, standard actions can be used to perform dynamic resource inclusion, include applets, forward response-processing requests, and include JavaBeans. Standard actions use an XML-like syntax with a start tag and an end tag. Some actions have body content, while others only have attributes. Not counting the standard actions used to write a JSP using XML notation, there are 13 standard actions. They are listed in Table 2.3 and detailed in the sections that follow.

2.8.1   JavaBean Standard Actions

JavaBeans were introduced into the Java programming language to enable component-based programming. Component-based programming was popularized with graphical programming tools in which different graphical components, such as a button, label, or panel, are combined to form a more complicated component. All interactions between any single component and other components are controlled via a well-defined interface, which greatly simplifies the development process. In Web applications, the component model

Standard Action	Summary
jsp:useBean	Create JavaBean object.
jsp:getProperty	Set a JavaBean property.
jsp:setProperty	Access a JavaBean property.
jsp:include	Dynamic include of a resource.
jsp:forward	Forward a request.
jsp:params	Wrap multiple parameters.
jsp:param	Specify request parameter.
jsp:plugin	Request Java Plugin.
jsp:fallback	Action to take if Java Plugin request fails.
jsp:invoke	Invoke JSP fragment.
jsp:doBody	Do Tag body.
jsp:attribute	Pass Tag attribute.
jsp:body	Pass Tag body.

Table 2.3: The JSP standard actions.

has also proven useful. When it is used, information, such as a user's credentials or a shopping cart, can be treated as a component shared among different resources.

A JavaBean is a class that provides an implementation for a specific component. Access to specific data within a Bean is controlled by get/set methods, in which the full name following the get/set prefix is the name of the target datum. For example, if a JavaBean has an integer variable called id, the JavaBean will have methods called getId and setId that provide access to the id variable.

There are three standard actions that implement JavaBean functionality within JSP pages: jsp:useBean, jsp:getProperty, and jsp:setProperty. Although JavaBeans and JSP pages are fully discussed in Chapter 3, the rest of this section discusses these three actions in more detail.

The jsp:useBean action is used within a JSP page to create a new scripting variable that is an instance of a JavaBean. In this sense, it can be thought of as a component declaration. The jsp:useBean action has five attributes:

- The id attribute is a case-sensitive name used to identify the object instantiated from the JavaBean class. This object is assigned to a scripting variable within the current JSP page that can then be used to directly access the JavaBean.

- The scope attribute defines the visibility of the newly instantiated object. This attribute can only be assigned one of the four legal scope values defined previously.

- The class attribute is the fully qualified class name that provides the actual implementation of the target JavaBean.

- The beanName attribute is a JavaBean that can be used by the instantiate method of the java.beans.Beans class. This attribute can be dynamically specified during the processing of a specific request, which may, in certain circumstances, provide more flexibility than the static approach of specifying the class name using the class attribute.

- The type attribute defines the actual type of scripting variable that is created. In object hierarchies, an object reference can be assigned to either its class, a super-class of the class, or an interface implemented by the class. This allows a developer to create a Bean that is only related, and not identical, to the class that is actually created. Combined with a dynamic use of the beanName attribute, this approach allows new JavaBeans to be dynamically added to provide polymorphic behavior (such as an updated shopping-cart class).

A jsp:useBean action can have an empty body, or it can have a body that consists of jsp:setProperty actions that assign values directly to the newly created Bean. Typically this is done directly from request parameters. The jsp:setProperty action can also be used on its own to change the state of a particular JavaBean. The jsp:setProperty action has four attributes:

- The name attribute is the name of the Bean as specified by the jsp:useBean id attribute.

- The property attribute is the name of the Bean property (or variable) that should be modified. Using the wildcard character * as the value of the property attribute causes the JSP container to match request parameters directly to identically named Bean properties.

- The param attribute names a request parameter that should be used as the value assigned to the specific property of the named Bean. The param attribute cannot be used in conjunction with the value attribute.

- The value attribute is the actual value that should be assigned to the specific property of the named Bean. The value attribute can be used to assign dynamically evaluated expressions and cannot be used in conjunction with the param attribute.

The following example demonstrates the use of these two actions to create a JavaBean and initialize its properties directly from the request object.

```
<jsp:useBean id="user" scope="session" class="com.persistentjava.LoginBean">
  <jsp:setProperty name="user" property="name" param="username"/>
  <jsp:setProperty name="user" property="passwd" param="password"/>
</jsp:useBean>
```

To access the properties of a JavaBean, you use the jsp:getProperty action, which converts the property to a String value and places it into the output stream. If an attempt is made to access the properties of a JavaBean that is not accessible (for example, it may be out of scope), a run-time exception will be thrown. The `jsp:getProperty` action takes two attributes:

- The name attribute is the name of the target JavaBean as specified by the relevant `jsp:useBean` id attribute.

- The property attribute is the name of the target property that should be accessed.

The following action demonstrates accessing the JavaBean created in the previous example.

```
<jsp:getProperty name="user" property="name"/>
```

2.8.2 Resource Actions

Six actions—`jsp:include`, `jsp:forward`, `jsp:params`, `jsp:param`, `jsp:plugin`, and `jsp:fallback`—are related to request processing.

The `jsp:param` action encapsulates a key/value pair that can be used in the body of a `jsp:include`, a `jsp:forward`, and a `jsp:params` action. When used with an `jsp:include` or `jsp:forward` action, the `jsp:param` data is added to the request object. Any existing information with the same name has lower precedence over the new data within the new resource. The `jsp:param` action has two attributes:

- The name attribute provides the name of the parameter.

- The value attribute provides the value associated with the provided name. The value attribute can be evaluated at request-time.

The `jsp:include` action can be used to incorporate both static and dynamic resources into the current JSP page. When adding a JSP page into the current JSP page, processing leaves the current page and starts with the new JSP page. The new JSP page only has access to the out implicit object and is unable to set HTTP headers, so it cannot, for example, set cookies. Once the new JSP page has been processed, the JSP container resumes processing the original JSP page. Request parameters can be modified for the included JSP page by adding appropriate `jsp:param` actions to the body of the `jsp:include` action. The `jsp:include` action takes two attributes:

- The page attribute is the URL for the resource to be included. Relative paths are evaluated relative to the current JSP page. The value of the page attribute can be dynamically evaluated at run-time.

- The flush attribute is a Boolean attribute that specifies whether the buffer is flushed before the resource is included (true) or not (false). The default value is false.

The following example demonstrates including a standard footer.

```
<jsp:include page="footer.jsp"/>
```

The next example demonstrates including a processing page that is passed new HTTP request parameters. The target page is determined at run-time from the target variable.

```
<jsp:include page="<%= target %>">
 <jsp:param name="user" value="joe"/>
 <jsp:param name="passwd" value="qw3rt7"/>
</jsp:include>
```

The jsp:forward action can be used to dispatch a request to a new resource. In effect, the JSP container stops processing the current JSP page and starts processing the new resource. Request parameters can be modified for the new resource by including jsp:param actions in the body of the jsp:forward action. If the current JSP page is buffered, the buffer is cleared before the request is forwarded. If the buffer has been flushed (data has been returned to the client), an IllegalStateException is thrown. The jsp:forward action takes one attribute:

- The page attribute is the URL for the resource that will handle the forwarded request. Relative paths are evaluated relative to the current JSP page. The value of the page attribute can be dynamically evaluated at run-time.

The following example demonstrates forwarding a request to another JSP page.

```
<jsp:forward page="new.jsp"/>
```

The next example demonstrates forwarding a request to a new page and adding new request parameters.

```
<jsp:forward page="new.jsp">
 <jsp:param name="user" value="joe"/>
 <jsp:param name="passwd" value="qw3rt7"/>
</jsp: forward >
```

The jsp:plugin action can be used to direct the JSP container to generate the client-specific HTML code required to download the Java Plugin software, if necessary, and to subsequently execute the indicated Applet or JavaBean component. The jsp:plugin action takes several attributes that control the appearance of the generated HTML,[10] including code, codebase, align, archive, height, hspace, name, vspace, title, and width. The jsp:plugin action also takes the following four attributes:

- The type attribute specifies whether the plugin is a Java Applet (applet) or a JavaBean component (bean).

- The jreversion identifies the Java Runtime Environment (JRE) version required by the plugin.

---

[10]For more information on these attributes, see the HTML specification at *http://www.w3.org/TR/html4*.

- The nspluginurl attribute specifies where the JRE plugin for Netscape clients can be downloaded.

- The iepluginurl attribute specifies where the JRE plugin for Internet Explorer clients can be downloaded.

The jsp:params action can only be used within the body of a jsp:plugin action, and it has no attributes. This action is used to group together one or more parameters, which are specified by the jsp:param action described previously, for use by the target of the jsp:plugin action.

The jsp:fallback action provides the content that should be used if the jsp:plugin action either is unable to be performed or fails to perform. Typically this would be a simple message stating that the plugin was unable to start. The jsp:fallback action has no attributes, and any message is supplied via the body of the jsp:fallback action.

Using the plugin and related actions is simple and is demonstrated in the following example, which tells the JSP compiler to generate the browser-relevant HTML code to display a mortgage calculator applet. Parameters are passed to the applet to indicate length of mortgage in years and the interest rate. Finally, a suitable message is displayed if the applet cannot be started or displayed by the client.

```
<jsp:plugin type="applet" code="MortgageCalculator.class">
 <jsp:params>
  <jsp:param name="irate" value="6.875"/>
  <jsp:param name="term" value="30"/>
 </jsp:params>
 <jsp:feedback>
  <p> The Mortgage Calculator was unable to start properly.
  <p> Please upgrade your browser and try again.
 </jsp:feedback>
</jsp:plugin>
```

2.8.3 Advanced Actions

The rest of the standard actions are more advanced in nature and are either used to encode a JSP document in XML syntax or to provide functionality required for a new concept in JSP development: JSP *Fragments*. For completeness, the JSP standard actions related to XML syntax are jsp:element, jsp:text, jsp:output, jsp:root, jsp:declaration, jsp:expression, and jsp:scriptlet. These actions allow a JSP document to be written using a standard XML syntax and are most likely to be of interest to JSP tool developers.

JSP fragments are small sections of JSP code encapsulated in an object that implements the javax.servlet.jsp.tagext.JspFragment interface. Fragments are discussed in more detail in Chapter 6, in which both jsp:invoke and jsp:doBody actions are detailed. Although jsp:attribute and jsp:body can be used with JSP fragments, they also provide additional functionality.

The jsp:attribute action can be used to pass an attribute to another action in the body of the action, rather than as a normal attribute. This action can be used for any attribute, but it often finds use when passing a JSP fragment to the target action. The jsp:attribute action accepts two attributes:

- The name attribute is the actual name for the attribute expected for the target action.

- The trim attribute is a Boolean attribute that indicates whether leading and trailing white space should be ignored (true) or not (false) when processing the body of the jsp:attribute action.

To demonstrate how this action can be used, consider the following simple action invocation.

```
<pjBank:aTag rate="6.875"/>
```

We can rewrite this using the jsp:attribute action, which places the attribute into the body of the action.

```
<pjBank:aTag>
 <jsp:attribute name="rate" trim="true">
  6.875
 </jsp:attribute>
</pjBank:aTag>
```

The jsp:body action works in a similar fashion to the jsp:attribute action. It wraps the body content of an action in a standard action. When the body of an action has been augmented with the jsp:attribute action, the original body content must be wrapped so the JSP container can identify it. The jsp:body action takes a single attribute, value, which is optional, and it allows the body content to be placed in an attribute rather than in the body of the jsp:body action.

To demonstrate how this action can be used, consider the following simple action invocation in which a custom tag named aTag from the pjBank tag library is invoked.

```
<pjBank:aTag rate="6.875">
 30
</pjBank:aTag>
```

We can rewrite this using the jsp:body action, which is necessary when we use the jsp:attribute action.

```
<pjBank:aTag>
 <jsp:attribute name="rate" trim="true">
  6.875
 </jsp:attribute>
 <jsp:body>
  30
 </jsp:body>
</pjBank:aTag>
```

We can also rewrite the jsp:body line in this example using the value attribute.

```
<jsp:body value="30"/>
```

Exercises

1. Name and describe as many attributes for the page directive as you can.

2. Describe, in your own words, the different scope levels defined in the JSP specification.

3. Given a JavaBean named PersonBean, with properties name, age, and gender, write a custom action that demonstrates using this Bean and setting all of its properties.

4. Describe the difference between variables declared in a JSP declaration element and those declared in a JSP scriptlet.

5. Write a simple JSP page that uses a scriptlet to generate an HTML table that displays a multiplication table. You can limit the size of the table to 10 by 10.

6. Name at least three implicit objects and describe how they can be used within a JSP page.

7. Describe the differences between the include directive and the include action.

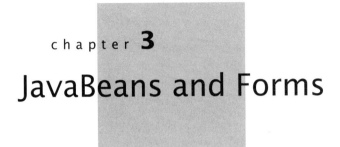

chapter **3**

JavaBeans and Forms

To this point, we have worked only with static content: a client makes a request and a standard response is generated. The real Web is obviously much more dynamic in nature than this simple approach, and JavaServer Page technology provides a wealth of support for producing dynamic Web applications. In this chapter, we will introduce *forms* as a mechanism for transmitting dynamic information as part of the client request. Following that, JavaBeans are presented and combined with Hypertext Markup language (HTML) forms to simplify dynamic Web applications. This chapter concludes with an example application that demonstrates building a simple dynamic Web application.

3.1 HTML Forms

The standard method for building a Web site is to present HTML pages to a client. The client can navigate through the HTML pages by clicking hyperlinks and using the browser's "back" button. While this model is useful for some application domains, a more interactive model is required for many domains, including e-commerce.

Fortunately, the World Wide Web Consortium (W3C) has included the form element within their HTML (and XHTML) recommendations. The form element and the related form controls allow a developer to obtain a variety of information, which is sent back to the server. This data can be used to generate dynamic Web pages, which are customized for a client based on the input data.

3.1.1 An Overview of HTML Forms

An HTML, or XHTML, form is created using the form element.[1] This element wraps the desired form controls into a single construct, which is encapsulated between the form's start and end tags. The form element takes several arguments, which control the overall behavior of the form. Of these attributes, the three most commonly used are name, action, and method. Other attributes can be used for controlling the presentation of the form, specifying what happens when certain events occur (for example, when the "submit" button is clicked), and defining the actual processing behavior of the server.

The name attribute provides a unique name for the form. This can be used at the Web server to access the data submitted by the form. The action attribute, which is required, specifies what should be done when the form is submitted. Typically this attribute specifies a Universal Resource Indicator (URI) that will process the form data (for example, account.jsp). The method attribute specifies what Hypertext Transport Protocol (HTTP) transport method—GET or POST—should be used to submit the form data.

The GET method, which is the default value, will append the data to the URI specified by the action attribute. Because Web browsers and servers can support different Universal Resource Locator (URL) maximum lengths, the GET method should not be used for large quantities of data; a good rule is to stay below 100 characters. The POST method, on the other hand, includes the form data as part of the body of the HTTP request. However, the POST method does not work with bookmarks.

The actual work in an HTML form is accomplished by controls. A *control* is a specific mechanism for obtaining input from the user. The different controls can be globally categorized as follows:

- *Button*: A button control comes in three flavors: submit, reset, and push. A button control can be created using the input or button elements.

- *Checkbox*: A checkbox control can take two values: on or off. Checkbox controls are created using the input element and can be grouped together by having multiple controls share the same name. This enables a single control name to have multiple values.

- *Radio Button*: A radio button control can take two values: on or off. Radio button controls are created using the input element and can be grouped together by having multiple controls share the same name. In the case of grouped radio button controls, however, only one radio button in the group can selected, or on.

- *Menu*: A menu control, or a drop-down list, allows multiple options to be presented in minimal space. The menu control is created using the select, option, and optgroup elements.

- *Text Input*: A text input control allows a user to enter arbitrary text. The input element can be used to create a single-line text input control, which is useful for entering a

---

[1]The full specification for HTML forms is available at *http://www.w3.org/TR/html4/interact/forms.html*.

limited amount of information. A textarea element can be used to create a multiline text input control, which is useful when a user may need to enter a large amount of information.

- *File Select*: A file select control allows a user to select files whose contents will be submitted as part of the form. The input element can be used to create a file select control.

- *Hidden*: A hidden control is not visible to the user and is used to pass information between the client and the server. This information sharing is not directly supported in HTTP because it is a stateless protocol. The input element is used to create a hidden control.

- *Object*: The object control, which is created with the input element, can be used to submit more complicated data with the form. Further discussion of this control is beyond the scope of this book.

After glancing at this list, you may notice that most controls are created using the input element. The behavior of this element is completely specified using attributes, but even though it has no body content, it does not take an end tag (thus, it is not well-formed XML!). While the input element accepts a large number of attributes, the most commonly used are type, name, and value.

The name and value attributes simply provide the name for the control and an initial value. The type attribute determines what type of control will be created. Legal values for the type attribute are as follows:

- text for a single-line text input control

- password for a single-line text input control that hides any characters entered by the user

- checkbox for a checkbox control

- radio for a radio button control

- submit for a button control that, when clicked, will submit the contents of the form to the URI specified in the form element's action attribute

- reset for a button control that, when clicked, will reset the contents of the form to their initial values

- file for a file select control

- hidden for a hidden control

- image for a button control that displays an image over the button and, when clicked, will submit the contents of the form to the URI specified in the form element's action attribute

- button for a generic button control that can be used to execute different client-side scripts depending on what the user does

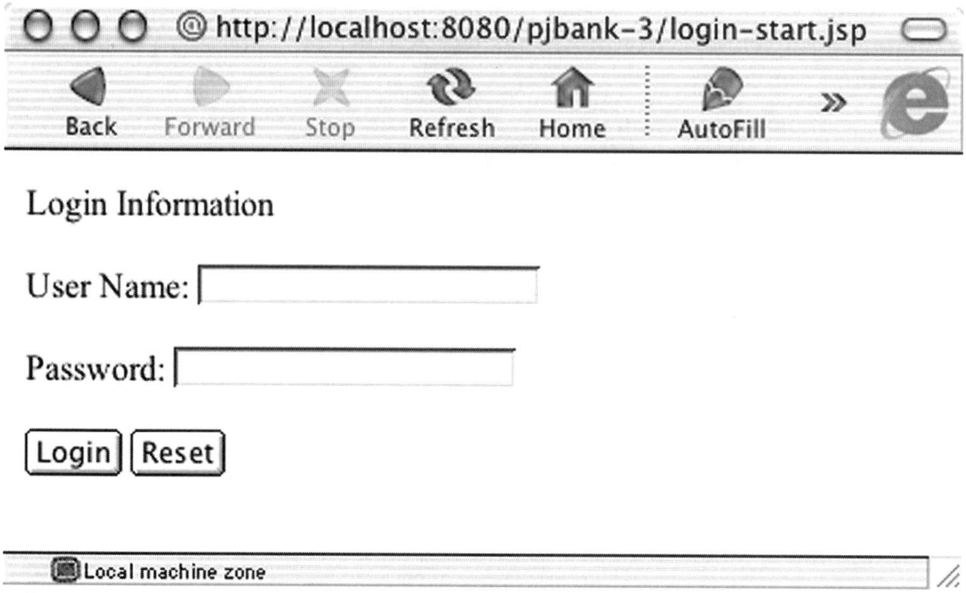

Figure 3.1: The rendered version of `login-start.jsp`.

Depending on the value of the type attribute, other attributes, such as size, maxlength, and checked, are also commonly used to control the behavior of the target control.

To demonstrate building a usable HTML form, and especially the utility of the input element, consider building a login form, as displayed in Figure 3.1. The controls typically required are the login name, the login password, a button to submit the information, and a reset button to clear any entered text. A complete HTML Web page that contains these login controls is shown as `login-start.jsp`.

Example 3.1 login-start.jsp

```
<html>
 <body>
  <form>
   Login Information
    <p/>User Name: <input type="text" name ="username">
    <p/>Password: <input type="password" name ="password">
    <p/><input type="submit" value="Login">
       <input type="reset">
  </form>
 </body>
</html>
```

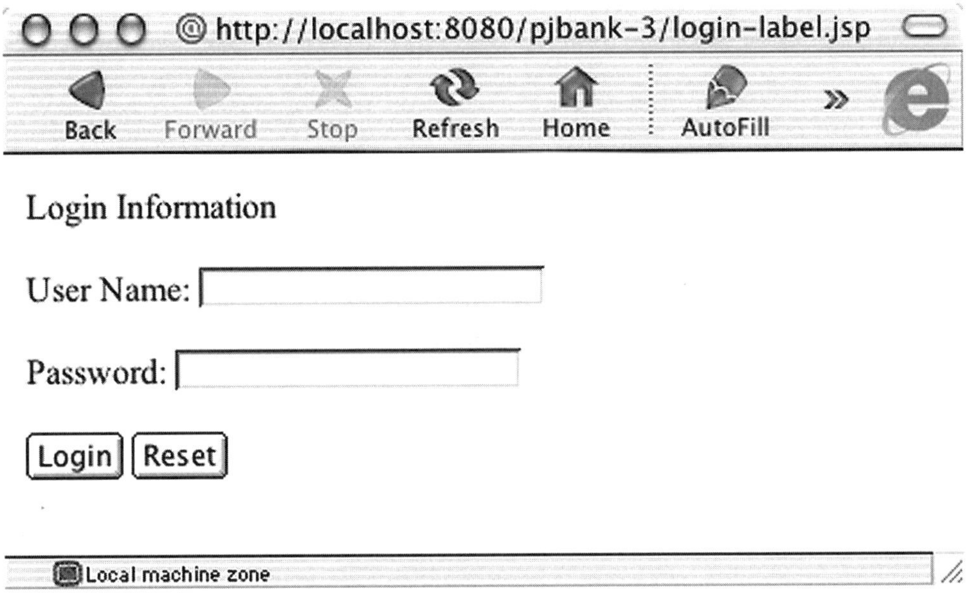

Figure 3.2: The rendered version of login-label.jsp.

While functional, this initial login Web page can be improved. The first item to tackle is the labels used to indicate the nature of the two text controls. While regular text can be used, the proper technique is to use the label element, which provides greater flexibility to the rendering agent. For example, different clients could transform the label element into spoken text or perhaps a tool tip.

A label element can be explicitly associated with a control by placing the control inside the body of the label element. Using this technique, we can convert our initial login form to use the label element, as shown in login-label.jsp. While the appearance of the Web page has not changed, as can be seen by comparing Figure 3.1 and Figure 3.2, our new version offers greater functionality by explicitly denoting the label text, which enables it to be processed as desired by the client.

Example 3.2 login-label.jsp

```
<html>
 <body>
  <form>
   Login Information
   <p/><label>User Name: <input type="text" name ="username"></label>
   <p/><label>Password: <input type="password" name ="password"></label>
   <p/><input type="submit" value="Login">
    <input type="reset">
```

```
  </form>
  </body>
</html>
```

Web pages are often filled with information, and directing the user to relevant information can sometimes be difficult. We can, however, improve the organization of this login page by using the `fieldset` element, as shown in `login-fieldset.jsp`. In this case, we only have to wrap the login form information inside a fieldset and move the form title into the body of a legend element. This assists the reader in focusing on the relevant tasks, in this case logging into the system, in what could be a Web page that contains many other components. As shown in Figure 3.3, all our login controls are nicely grouped together on the Web page.

One final change we can make is to wrap the form input text fields inside an HTML table. This allows the page author to easily control how everything is laid out on the Web page. For example, you may notice that the user and password text fields in our login example are not aligned. Placing them in table cells would force them to be aligned. However,

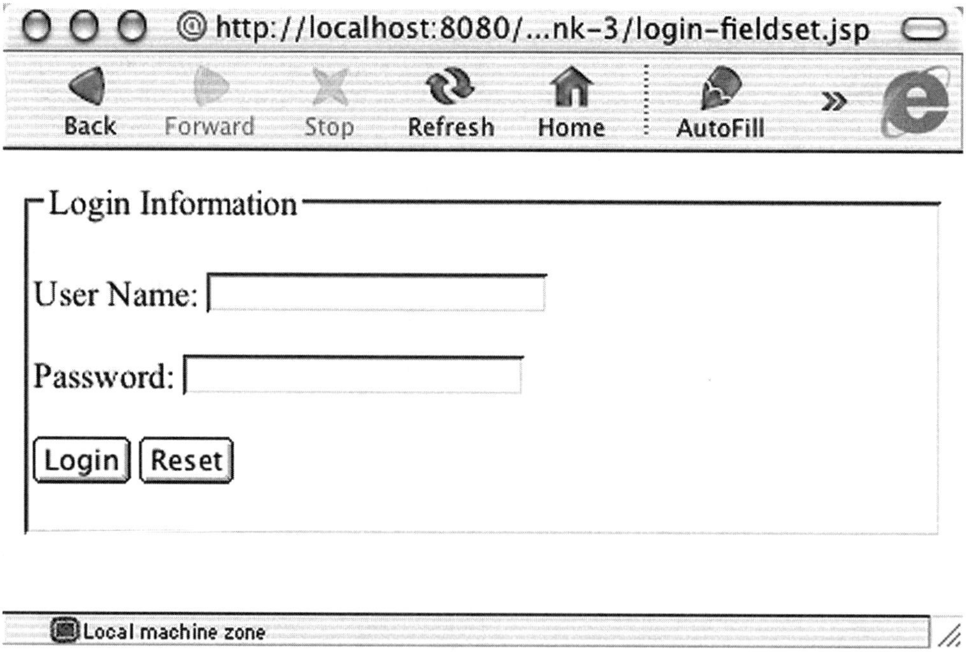

Figure 3.3: The rendered version of `login-fieldset.jsp`.

Example 3.3 login-fieldset.jsp

```
<html>
 <body>
  <form>
   <fieldset>
    <legend>Login Information</legend>
    <p/><label>User Name: <input type="text" name ="username"></label>
    <p/><label>Password: <input type="password" name ="password"></label>
    <p/><input type="submit" value="Login">
     <input type="reset">
   </fieldset>
  </form>
 </body>
</html>
```

this complicates the use of our label elements. The solution is to place the label elements in one column and the text fields in a separate column. We can use an id attribute with each input element to associate our label elements with the appropriate input element, as shown in login-final.jsp. As Figure 3.4 demonstrates, the text controls are now nicely aligned.

Figure 3.4: The rendered version of login-final.jsp.

Example 3.4 login-final.jsp

```
<html>
 <body>
  <form>
   <fieldset>
    <legend>Login Information</legend>
    <table>
     <tr>
      <td><label for="uname">User Name:</label></td>
      <td><input type="text" name="username" id="uname"></td>
     </tr>
     <tr>
      <td><label for="pword">Password:</label></td>
      <td><input type="password" name ="password" id="pword"></td>
     </tr>
    </table>
    <p/><input type="submit" value="Login">
        <input type="reset">
   </fieldset>
  </form>
 </body>
</html>
```

At this point, we have glossed over several important points regarding HTML forms. First, the various login form examples did not define any action attributes. As a result, no action was taken when the form data was submitted. Another interesting point is that these HTML forms were saved as JSP pages, yet they contained only HTML elements. This demonstrates the flexibility of JSP technology; you can include as much or as little dynamic content as you need in a page.

3.1.2 JSP Form Processing

Now that we have a basic form, the next step is to start processing the form data. Form data is passed to a JSP page as parameter data contained within the request object. The request object's getParameter method can be called to access form data. This method takes a string argument that is the name of the desired form control and returns the value of the target control as a String or as null if no value is present in the request. To demonstrate, login-process.jsp displays the data entered by any of the previous login JSP pages, as shown in Figure 3.5.

Example 3.5 login-process.jsp

```
<html>
 <body>
```

Figure 3.5: The rendered version of login-process.jsp.

```
<h2> Login Information </h2>
<hr/>
<h4> User Name: <%= request.getParameter("username") %> </h4>
<h4> Password : <%= request.getParameter("password") %> </h4>
<hr/>
</body>
</html>
```

To use this JSP page, the action attribute for any of the previous login forms should be set to login-process.jsp, as follows:

```
<form action="login-process.jsp">
```

Often, it is easiest to couple the form and its processing in a single JSP page fragment. This simplifies development because the form data is acquired and processed together. The only major change is that a JSP scriptlet needs to be used to determine whether to display the form or process the form data, as seen in login-all.jsp. One simple technique to solve this difficulty is to test whether a particular input control has been assigned a value (although in production you might instead rely on a validation script to set a Boolean flag).

Example 3.6 login-all.jsp

```
<html>
 <body>
<%
 String username = request.getParameter("username") ;
 if(username != null){ // Processing the Form data
%>
  <h2> Login Information </h2>
  <hr/>
  <h4> User Name: <%= username %>   </h4>
  <h4> Password : <%= request.getParameter("password") %> </h4>
  <hr/>
<%
 }else{ // Display the Form
%>
 <form>
  <fieldset>
   <legend>Login Information</legend>
   <table>
    <tr>
     <td><label for="uname">User Name:</label></td>
     <td><input type="text" name ="username" id="uname"></td>
    </tr>
    <tr>
     <td><label for="pword">Password:</label></td>
     <td><input type="password" name ="password" id="pword"></td>
    </tr>
   </table>
   <p/><input type="submit" value="Login">
        <input type="reset">
  </fieldset>
  </form>
<% } %>
 </body>
</html>
```

Although a JSP page is generally tightly coupled with a target form (because the form can either be generated by a JSP page or they can be coupled together as previously shown), sometimes a JSP page needs to determine available request parameters and their associated values dynamically.

    The first method to process arbitrary request parameters is to call the getParameter Names method to get a string array that contains the names of all request parameters, then call the getParameterValues method to get a string array that contains the values of all request parameters. The second approach is to call the getParameterMap method, which returns a java.util.Map object that uses the request parameter names as the Map keys and the request parameter values as the Map values. All of these methods can be called on the request object. The following example demonstrates how to grab all values associated with each request parameter.

```
String name ;
String[] values ;
Enumeration names = request.getParameterNames();
while(names.hasMoreElements()) {
 name = (String)names.nextElement();
 values = request.getParameterValues(name) ;
 // Do something with the Parameter name and associated values
}
```

3.1.3 An Email Form

Another form that can be useful when building a Web application is an email form. For now, we can focus on building a simple Web page that allows a reader to provide feedback, as shown in Figure 3.6. We will need multiple controls, including text, a check button, and radio button controls, to obtain the user's personal information (so we know who to contact); a menu control so the reader can select a standard subject line; and both "submit" and "reset" button controls. In a production system, the form should be submitted to a processing JSP page, but for now, we can hardcode the target email address within the value of the form element's action attribute, as shown in email-form.jsp.

Example 3.7 email-form.jsp

```
<html>
 <body>
  <form action="mailto:user@domain.com">
   <fieldset>
    <legend>Personal Information</legend>
    <table>
     <tr>
      <td><label for="fname">First Name</label></td>
      <td><input type="text" name ="fname" id="fname"></td>
     </tr>
     <tr>
      <td><label for="lname">Last Name</label></td>
      <td><input type="text" name ="lname" id="lname"></td>
     </tr>
     <tr>
      <td><label for="gender">Gender</label></td>
      <td>
       <input type="radio" name ="gender" id="gender" value="Male">
```

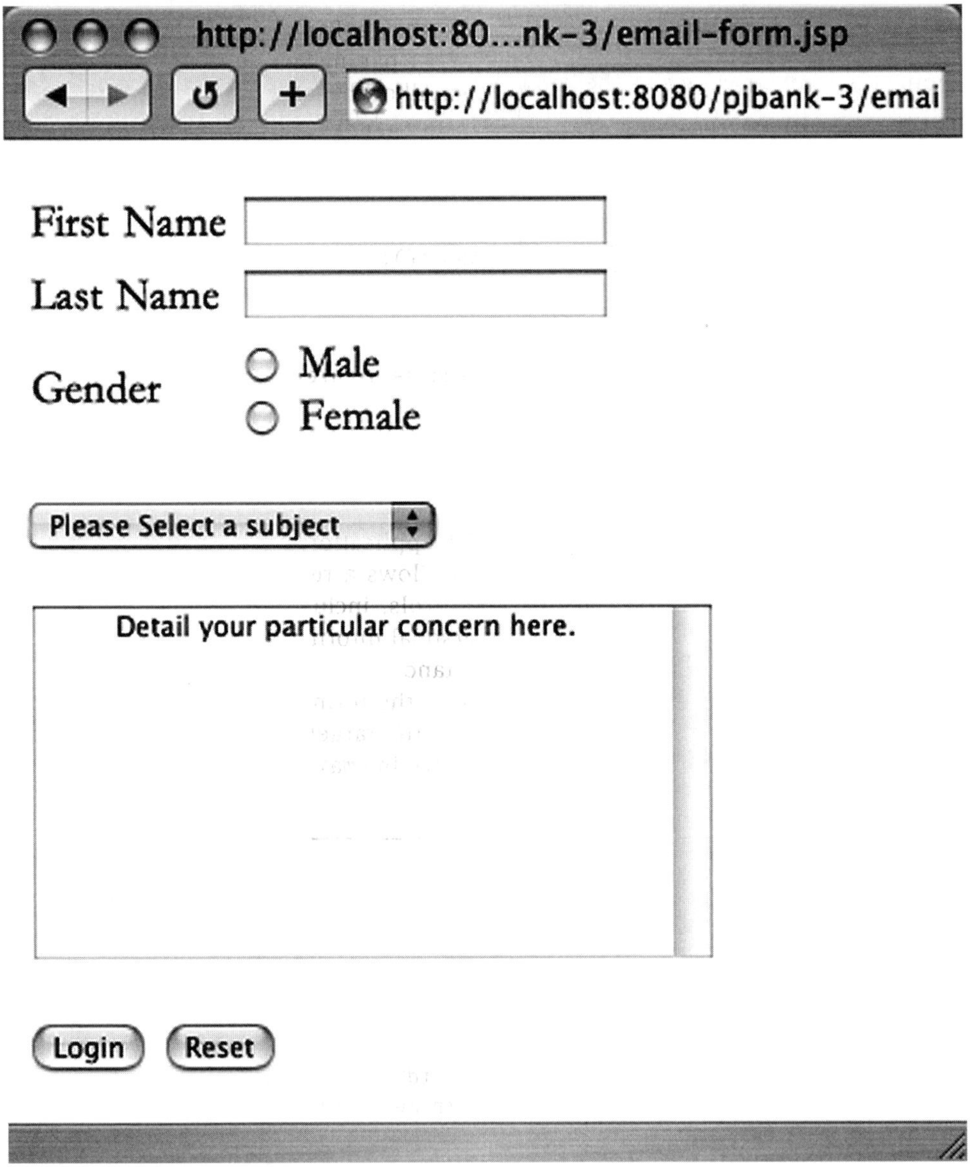

Figure 3.6: The rendered version of email-form.jsp.

```
      Male <br/>
      <input type="radio" name ="gender" id="gender" value="Female">
      Female <br/>
     </td>
    </tr>
   </table>
  </fieldset>
  <p/>
  <fieldset>
   <legend>Contact Information</legend>
   <select name="subject">
    <option selected="true" label="Please Select a subject"/>
    <option label="Can't access my accounts"/>
    <option label="Missing transaction"/>
    <option label="Balance dispute"/>
    <option label="Other"/>
   </select>
   <p/>
   <textarea name="message" rows="10" cols="40" id="body"
    onfocus="clear()">
    Detail your particular concern here.
   </textarea>
   <p/>
   <input type="submit" value="Login">
   <input type="reset">
  </fieldset>
 </form>
 </body>
</html>
```

Grabbing the form data directly from the request object may not seem overly complex; however, most Web applications involve multiple forms that are processed by a number of JSP pages. This can lead to unnecessary complications. Fortunately, the JSP specification provides a solution, described in the next section, via the integration of JavaBeans within a JSP page.

3.2 JavaBeans

Formally, a JavaBean[2] is a reusable software component written in Java. While this might sound confusing, the concept is simple. A JavaBean wraps a collection of related properties

---

[2]The official homepage for JavaBean technology is *http://java.sun.com/products/javabeans.*

together, provides controlled access to the properties, and dictates how the properties will respond to specific events. The properties encased within the JavaBean can be simple data, such as names and passwords, or more complex data, such as the properties of a button or menu item.

3.2.1   Bean Basics

A JavaBean can basically be considered a property container. The property values are declared private and can only be accessed by special methods, known as *getters* and *setters*. To read a specific property, you call getProperty. On the other hand, to write a specific property, you call setProperty. To be a good JavaBean, these methods must follow a special naming scheme in which the *Property* in the *get* and *set* methods is replaced by the name of the actual property. For example, the following listing demonstrates a simple JavaBean that contains a single property called title.

Example 3.8 TitleBean.java

```
package com.pjbank;

public class TitleBean
{
  private String title ;

  public TitleBean() {
  }

  public String getTitle() {
    return title ;
  }

  public void setTitle(String value) {
    title = value ;
  }
}
```

This simple class demonstrates a couple of important points about a JavaBean. First, while not required, it is a good idea to end the name of a JavaBean with the word *Bean*. This quickly conveys to anyone reading your code that this class is a JavaBean. Second, the encapsulation of the title property is fairly clear, as the only access is through the relevant get and set methods. Third, and an important item for JSP developers, a JavaBean that will be used within a JSP application must have an empty, or null, constructor.

A common question when looking at a JavaBean such as TitleBean is: Why even bother? After all, the get and set methods do not do anything other than provide direct access to the property. The simple response is that by decoupling the `title` property from the code that uses the property, the resulting code becomes easier to maintain. For example, suppose that `TitleBean` is modified so the `title` property is pulled out of a database in the `getTitle` method, and the `setTitle` method actually updates the database. Any code written to use the `TitleBean` will still work.

TitleBean only contained a single string property. A JavaBean can contain numerous different properties, which can each be a different Java datatype. A JavaBean can also contain indexed properties. The only real complexity added to handle indexed properties is that separate get and set methods have to be written not only to access the entire collection, but also to access a single property from the collection. Thus, if we have a JavaBean that contains an array of strings (called *titles*), we would need the following four methods:

- `public String getTitles(int index)`
- `public String[] getTitles()`
- `public void setTitles(int index, String title)`
- `public void setTitles(String[] titles)`

where `index` is the relevant index number for the desired title in the collection of titles.

In the example JSP pages shown earlier in this chapter, two properties were collected from the client: *username* and *password*. These properties can be collected into a JavaBean, as shown in LoginBean.java. An extra property, the Boolean valid property, has been included in this JavaBean. This property can be used to indicate whether the login data represents a valid user. In this simple demonstration, a valid login is indicated by a non-null username and password. In a production environment, however, this information could be validated against a database or local cache. Notice that this JavaBean implements the Serializable interface. This allows the JavaBean to be shared between different components of a Web application, even between server restarts.

Example 3.9 LoginBean.java

```java
package com.pjbank ;

import java.io.Serializable;

public class LoginBean implements Serializable {

  private String username ;
  private String password ;
  private boolean valid = false ;

  public LoginBean() {
  }
```

```
public String getUsername() {
  return username;
}

public void setUsername(String value) {
  username = value ;
}

public String getPassword() {
  return password;
}

public void setPassword(String value) {
  password = value ;
}

public boolean isValid() {

  valid=false ; // By default assume invalid login attempt

  if((username != null)&&(password != null))
    valid = true ;
  return valid ;
  }
}
```

3.2.2 JavaBeans and Forms

While we can create any Java object, including a JavaBean, in a JSP scriptlet, the JSP specification provides three custom actions that simplify the use of a JavaBean from within a JSP page. These three actions—jsp:useBean, jsp:setProperty, and jsp:getProperty—were detailed in Chapter 2. Together, they simplify using a JavaBean within a JSP page considerably. The useBean action is used to create (or reference a previously created) JavaBean; the getProperty action is used to get a specific property from a named JavaBean; and the setProperty action is used to set a specific property from a named JavaBean. Although the useBean action must precede the other two, these actions can appear anywhere in the page. However, it is generally considered good practice to place them immediately after the page directive.

An additional benefit of using the setProperty action is that a JSP container can be directed to automatically map request attributes to the properties of a JavaBean. The only requirement for this magic is that the request attribute and the JavaBean property must have the same name. This useful shortcut is indicated by using the asterisk character (*) as the value of the property attribute in the setProperty action.

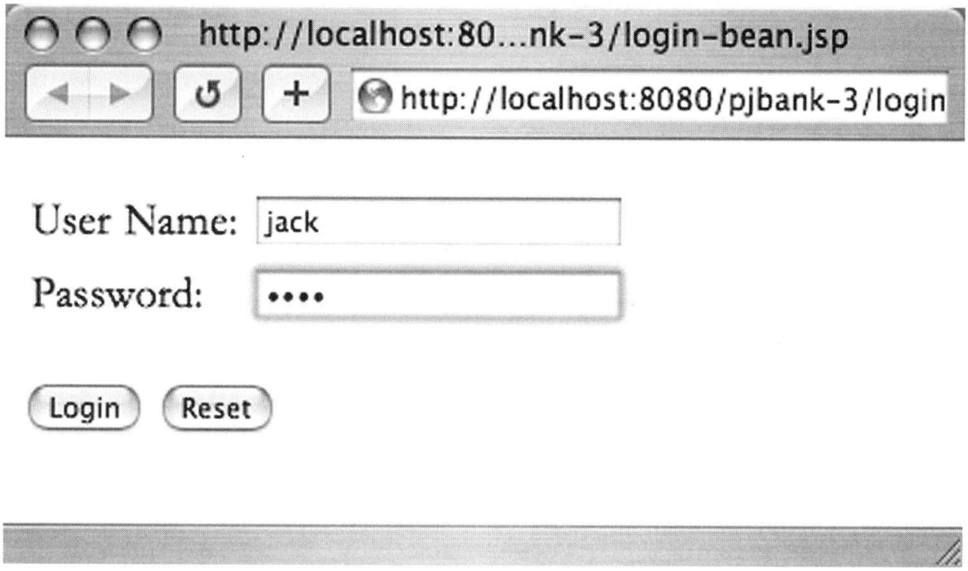

Figure 3.7: The rendered version of `login-bean.jsp`.

The `login-bean.jsp` below shows how the LoginBean JavaBean can be used within a login JSP page, as shown in Figure 3.7.

Example 3.10 login-bean.jsp

```jsp
<%@ page errorPage="exception.jsp" %>

<jsp:useBean id="login" class="com.pjbank.LoginBean" scope="session"/>
<jsp:setProperty name="login" property="*"/>

<html>
 <body>
<%
 if(login.getUsername() != null){ // Processing the Form data
%>
  <h2> Login Information </h2>
  <hr/>
  <h4> User Name: <jsp:getProperty name="login" property="username"/> </h4>
  <h4> Password : <jsp:getProperty name="login" property="password"/> </h4>
  <hr/>
<jsp:setProperty name="login" property="username" value="" />
<%
```

```
login.setPassword("") ;

}else{ // Display the Form
%>
  <form>
   <fieldset>
    <legend>Login Information</legend>
    <table>
     <tr>
      <td><label for="username">User Name:</label></td>
      <td><input type="text" name ="username" id="username"></td>
     </tr>
     <tr>
      <td><label for="password">Password:</label></td>
      <td><input type="password" name ="password" id="password"></td>
     </tr>
    </table>
    <p/><input type="submit" value="Login">
     <input type="reset">
   </fieldset>
  </form>
<% } %>
 </body>
</html>
```

This JSP page demonstrates several different concepts. First, the LoginBean is created using the useBean action. The fully qualified name for the JavaBean is assigned to the class attribute, the bean is named using the id attribute, and the scope attribute is used to specify that the newly created JavaBean will have session scope. Once our LoginBean has been created, it can be used. The setProperty action initializes the LoginBean with the corresponding attributes from the request object.

To determine whether a login form should be displayed or not, the isValid method is called. Notice how the useBean action created a scripting variable named login that allows direct access to the JavaBean within a scriptlet. If the request contains a valid login, the user information is displayed using the getProperty action. This same affect could have been achieved using a JSP expression that uses the login variable to call the appropriate get method.

After displaying the user information, the Bean properties are reset. This is done using both the setProperty action, as well as a direct call to the setPassword method within a scriptlet. This reinitialization was done because the initial setProperty action was not contained within the body of the useBean action. As a result, every time this JSP page is processed, the LoginBean is reinitialized with the corresponding request attributes. The alternative is to place the initial setProperty action inside the useBean action. This instructs the JSP container to set the Bean properties only when the Bean is first created.

```
<jsp:useBean id="login" class="com.pjbank.LoginBean" scope="session">
  <jsp:setProperty name="login" property="*"/>
</jsp:useBean>
```

3.3 Simple Web Application

The previous examples have all been somewhat limited, as they were designed to demonstrate a specific concept or functionality. However, with just basic JSP concepts, JavaBeans and forms, a complicated Web site can actually be constructed. In this section, a Web site for a fictional bank, the Persistent Java Bank, is built. To demonstrate how all the different technologies come together for a dynamic Web site, Internationalization, Cascading Style Sheets (CSS), and JavaScript are used. Note that this example is designed to show how all of these different technologies work together and should not be considered a lesson in designing Web applications. Good design is an art in and of itself and is best done by those who posses that particular skill.

3.3.1 The Welcome Page

The start of the PJ Bank Web site is the welcome page. Among other approaches, one traditional HTML page-design technique is to break a page up into five areas: the header, footer, left banner, right banner, and main body. Typically, the main body is where content varies, depending on the request parameters or location within a Web site, while the other four areas are more consistent (with the exception of possible advertising or other targeted information). This layout is demonstrated in Figure 3.8.

For the PJ Bank application, the header, footer, and left and right banner areas are generated from separate JSP pages (in reality they are JSP fragments because they are not complete pages on their own). These four pages are included in welcome.jsp, which also contains the main body. The basics of this JSP page are rather straightforward. First, an error JSP page is specified, after which the header is included. The header is included using the include action, which means that the header is processed with every page request. The header page expects a parameter that specifies the desired title for the displayed Web page, which is communicated using the param standard action. The welcome page concludes by including the footer page with the include standard action.

After the header, a table is constructed that splits the page into three areas: left, main, and right. The left area is filled with the left-banner JSP page fragment, while the right is filled with the right-banner JSP page fragment. The left banner is included with the jsp include action, meaning it is processed with every page request, while the right banner is included with the include directive, meaning that it is only processed when the page

Welcome Page Layout

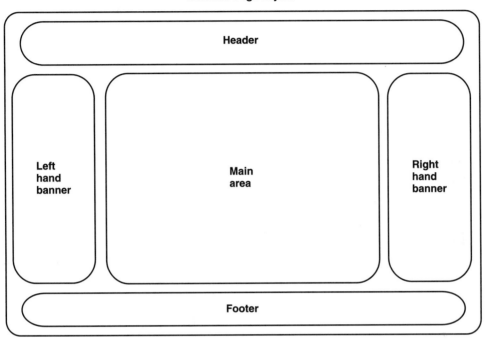

Figure 3.8: The five-panel layout for the Welcome page.

fragment is first included in the welcome JSP page. Notice that the different JSP fragment files use the *.jspf* file extension. The final result is shown in Figure 3.9.

Example 3.11 welcome.jsp

```
<%@ page contentType="text/html" errorPage="exception.jsp"%>
<jsp:include page="header.jspf">
 <jsp:param name="page-title" value="Welcome to PJ Bank"/>
</jsp:include>

<table width="100%">
 <tr>
  <td valign="top" width="25%"> <jsp:include page="left-banner.jspf" /> </td>
  <td valign="top">
   Welcome to PJ Bank, the persistent bank for those who like Java!
  </td>
  <td valign="top" width="25%"> <%@ include file="right-banner.jspf" %> </td>
 </tr>
```

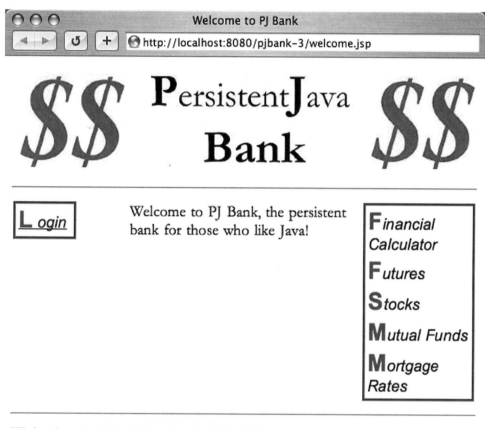

Figure 3.9: The rendered version of welcome.jsp.

```
</table>
<jsp:include page="footer.jspf"/>
```

To be a complete Web application, we need an error-handling JSP page, which for this application can be very simple. As shown in exception.jsp, the error page merely indicates that something went wrong. In a production system, this page might log a detailed message, send email to a help support group, or even try to recover from the situation.

Example 3.12 exception.jsp

```
<%@ page isErrorPage="true" %>
<html>
 <body>
  <h2> An error has occurred! </h2>
<% = exception.getMessage() %>
 </body>
</html>
```

The header is generated in header.jspf, which is designed to be functional across multiple Web pages. The header JSP page fragment is responsible for three actions. First, it links to both a JavaScript page and a stylesheet (these will be discussed more in Chapter 7), which are then available to any JSP page that includes this header page fragment. Second, it generates the HTML title element. To make the header more dynamic, a request parameter is used to pass a page title between the parent page and the header page fragment. Finally, the header page displays the bank's logo image, which in this case is rather simple. An actual graphic artist should be contracted for a production system.

Example 3.13 header.jspf

```
<html>
 <head>
  <script src='scripts/login.js'></script>
  <link rel="stylesheet" type="text/css" href="style/pjbank.css"/>
  <title><%= request.getParameter("page-title") %></title>
 </head>

 <body>
  <img src="images/banner.jpg" width="100%"
   alt="PersistentJava Bank Banner Image"/>

  <hr/>
```

Unlike a header, many footer JSP page fragments are rather static. For the PJ Bank application, the footer JSP page wraps up the HTML body and displays the current date followed by a copyright notice. To make matters more interesting, the date is generated dynamically and formatted according to the client's locale. A locale can be specific to a client's country, language, and culture and is indicated using a language[3] and

---

[3]The language code standard is available at *http://www.oasis-open.org/cover/iso639a.html.*

country[4] code, both of which are International Standards Organization (ISO) standards.

This last part, formatting information according to a client's location, culture, and language, is becoming more important as Web sites cater to a wider range of more diverse clients. This process requires the introduction of two new concepts, *Internationalization*, often abbreviated as i18n,[5] and *Localization*, often abbreviated as l10n (the abbreviations are formed by using the first and last letter with the number of characters in the word in between). Internationalization is the process of making an application work with different languages and customs, such as displaying a date according to the client's preferred locale. Localization, on the other hand, is the process of identifying the relevant information within a Web site or application that is language- or culture-specific, such as how a date is formatted and displayed.

A client's browser communicates acceptable locales as part of the HTTP request. Two methods that are part of the request object provide direct access to this information. The first, getLocale, returns the client's preferred locale and is shown in footer.jspf. The second method, getLocales, returns an Enumeration of locales and allows a client to communicate a sequence of acceptable locales to a server. This allows a server to identify a common locale on which both the client and server can agree.

The Java programming language contains a number of classes that simplify the internationalization and localization processes, including the Locale, DateFormat, and NumberFormat classes. The DateFormat class is demonstrated in footer.jspf, in which it is used to generate a string containing the current date and time, formatted according to the client's preferred locale. However, except for the discussion of the internationalization components in the JSP Standard Tag Library in Chapter 5, this subject is beyond the scope of this book.[6]

Example 3.14 footer.jspf

```
<%@ page import="java.text.DateFormat" %>
<%
 java.util.Locale lc = request.getLocale() ;
 java.util.Date dt = new java.util.Date() ;

 DateFormat df = DateFormat.getDateTimeInstance(DateFormat.FULL,
  DateFormat.FULL, lc) ;
%>

<hr/>
```

---

[4]The country code standard is available at *http://www.iso.ch/iso/en/prods-services/iso3166ma/index.html.*
[5]There are 18 characters between the starting "i" and the ending "n" in internationalization.
[6]The online Java Tutorial contains a gentle introduction to this subject at *http://java.sun.com/docs/books/tutorial/i18n.*

```
</body>
<address>
<% = df.format(dt) %>
<br/>
&copy; PJBank, 2002
</address>
</html>
```

The left-banner area must be dynamically processed with each page request because what is actually displayed varies depending on whether a client has successfully logged into the system. First, the LoginBean is created and initialized using the useBean and setProperty standard actions. An HTML table is created, and this example only has one row but more could easily be added. If the login is valid, the user is allowed to access his or her account. Otherwise, the user is given a link to the login page.

One additional point about this page fragment is the use of the class attribute with the HTML font element. This attribute will be used by the Web application's CSS, which is presented in full in Chapter 7, to specify formatting information specific to the element data. The particular styling chosen for this example is only meant to demonstrate how a style can be applied and is not intended as a good design choice.

Example 3.15 left-banner.jspf

```
<jsp:useBean id="login" class="com.pjbank.LoginBean" scope="session" />
<jsp:setProperty name="login" property="*" />

<table class="border">
<%
 if(login.isValid()) {
%>
 <tr><td>
  <font class="start">A</font>
  <font class="rest">Access Account</font>
 </td></tr>
<% }else { %>
 <tr><td>
  <a href="login.jsp">
  <font class="start">L</font>
  <font class="rest">Login</font>
  </a>
 </td></tr>
<% } %>
</table>
```

The right-banner area is static, merely a collection of links (in this simple demo the links are not included) to different financial areas that the fictitious PJ Bank supports for its clients. This data is collected in an HTML table and uses the class attribute to simplify the presentation of the data.

Example 3.16 right-banner.jspf

```
<table class="border">
 <tr><td>
   <font class="start">F</font><font class="rest">inancial Calculator</font>
 </td></tr>
 <tr><td>
   <font class="start">F</font><font class="rest">utures</font>
 </td></tr>
 <tr><td>
   <font class="start">S</font><font class="rest">tocks</font>
 </td></tr>
 <tr><td>
   <font class="start">M</font><font class="rest">utual Funds</font>
 </td></tr>
 <tr><td>
   <font class="start">M</font><font class="rest">ortgage Rates</font>
 </td></tr>
</table>
```

3.3.2 The Login Page

The last component of the initial PJ Bank Web application is the final login JSP page. Putting together everything that has been introduced in this chapter produces login.jsp.

Example 3.17 login.jsp

```
<%@ page contentType="text/html" errorPage="exception.jsp"%>

<jsp:useBean id="login" class="com.pjbank.LoginBean" scope="session"/>
<jsp:setProperty name="login" property="*"/>

<jsp:include page="header.jspf">
 <jsp:param name="page-title" value="Please Login"/>
</jsp:include>

<%
 String uname = "" ;
 String pword = "" ;
```

```
if(login.getUsername() != null){ // Processing the Form data

 uname = login.getUsername() ;
 pword = login.getPassword() ;
 }
%>
  <form action="welcome.jsp" method='post' name='loginForm'
   onsubmit='return validate()'>
   <fieldset>
    <legend>Login Information</legend>
    <table>
     <tr>
      <td><label for="username">User Name:</label></td>
      <td><input type="text" name ="username" id="username">
       <% = uname %></td>
     </tr>
     <tr>
      <td><label for="password">Password:</label></td>
      <td><input type="password" name ="password" id="password">
       <% = pword %></td>
     </tr>
    </table>
    <p/><input type="submit" value="Login">
    <input type="reset">
   </fieldset>
  </form>
 </body>
</html>
```

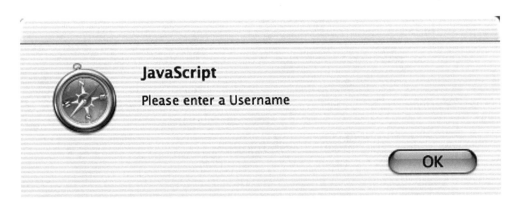

Figure 3.10: The alert window showing no username was entered.

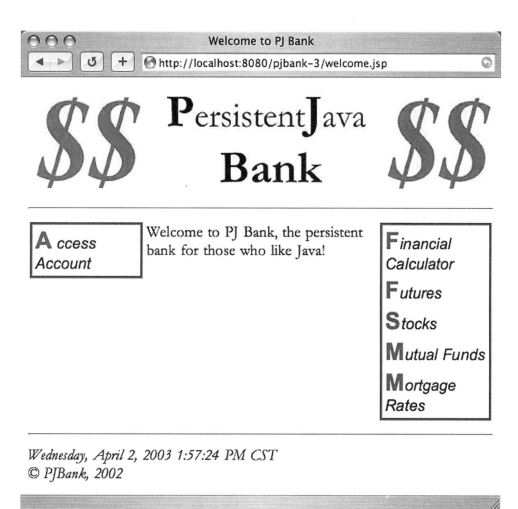

Figure 3.11: The rendered version of `welcome.jsp` after a successful login.

This JSP page displays the login form and provides default values if the user has already accessed this Web page via the JSP expressions. Before the form data is sent to the server, the validate JavaScript function is called. If the username or password is blank, an alert window, like the one shown in Figure 3.10, is displayed. Otherwise the data is sent to the server and the Welcome page is modified accordingly, as seen in Figure 3.11.

JavaScript is discussed in more detail in Chapter 7, in which the JavaScript validate method is presented.

Exercises

1. Name and describe four different form element controls.

2. Describe how to specify a target action for a form element.

3. Create an HTML page that contains a form element that has a text input control to specify quantity and a hidden control to specify an item number.

4. Create a JavaBean named ItemBean to hold an integer named itemNumber, a string named description, a BigDecimal named price, and an integer named quantity.

5. Create a JavaBean named ShoppingCartBean that contains ItemBean instances.

6. Create a JSP page that will be called from the HTML page you created in Exercise 3. The JSP page should create an ItemBean to hold the data submitted. Describe how the price and description values might be obtained in a production environment.

7. Identify localization targets in the JSP and HTML pages created in Exercises 3 and 6.

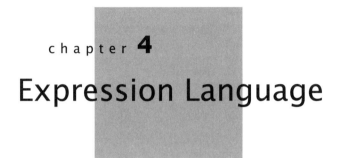

chapter **4**

Expression Language

In the last chapter, you were exposed to JavaServer Pages declarations, expressions, and scriptlets, all of which require a (sometimes detailed) knowledge of the Java programming language to be used effectively. This has two primary effects. First, it limits the pool of available developers, which is important because most Web developers do not know Java, and most Java programmers are not skilled in designing Web sites. Second, it complicates the long-term maintenance of Web applications, because the Java code may introduce additional dependencies, be poorly documented, or contain hidden bugs.

A primary goal of the JSP specification committee has been to allow developers to use JSP to quickly develop rich Web applications that are easy to deploy and maintain. One of the largest impediments to this goal has been the proliferation of Java code within JSP pages. The majority of Web developers are familiar with using tags explicitly, or implicitly via the availability of wizards and palettes from integrated development environments (IDEs). They also are likely to have some exposure to scripting languages, which are much less complicated and more forgiving than a full-feature programming language such as Java.

As a result, the JSP specification has evolved to support Java-free JSP pages. This support rests primarily in the JSP Expression Language (EL), the JSP Standard Tag Library (JSTL), and the ability to develop custom tags, or actions. This chapter will introduce the JSP EL, but JSTL will be covered in Chapter 5, and the development of custom tags will be presented in Chapter 6.

4.1   EL Overview

The JSP EL borrows ideas from other scripting languages, primarily ECMAScript[1] and the XPath[2] expression language, and is based on two main ideas. The first is that data access is done exclusively via scoped attributes, or variables. This allows expressions and tags within a JSP page to easily share data, without the complication of variable declarations. The second idea is that an expression is the fundamental building block. The following list details the different types of expressions:

- a literal value

- a scoped attribute

- a function call

- an arithmetic, relational, or logical operation involving a combination of the previous three items

The spirit of a scripting language is to be easy to use and is forgiving of potential errors. The JSP EL follows this ideal, as expressions can be used to specify attribute values and can be used within template text.[3] The JSP EL also provides automatic type coercion and default values that simplify the development of JSP documents. As an example, rather than throwing an exception when a scoped attribute has not been defined, the EL defaults to having a default value of null.

An EL expression is indicated in a JSP page by enclosing it within curly braces and prefixing it with a dollar sign. So, to specify an expression expr, you would add ${expr} to your JSP document. When used in template text, the expression is evaluated and inserted into the current output stream, which may be buffered. Expressions can be used to specify the value of an attribute for a JSP standard or custom action (tag) in three different ways:

- as a literal value, which is automatically type coerced to the attribute's target type:

      ```
      <pjbank:tag value="text" />
      ```

- as a single expression, which is evaluated and automatically type coerced to the attribute's target type:

      ```
      <pjbank:tag value="${expr}" />
      ```

---

[1]ECMAScript is the official JavaScript specification. The specification can be found online at *http://www.ecma-international.org/publications/standards/ECMA-262.HTM.*
[2]The XPath expression language specification can be found online at *http://www.w3.org/TR/xpath#section-Expressions.*
[3]Technically this is true only within JSP 2.0-compliant containers. To use an EL in containers that support earlier versions of the JSP specification, you must use the JSTL EL, which does not support expressions in template text.

- as multiple expressions enclosed within literal string values (or text) in which the expressions are evaluated in order from left to right, coerced to strings and concatenated with the literal strings. The end result is automatically type-coerced to the attribute's target type:

```
<pjbank:tag value="text${expr}more text${expr}${expr}more text" />
```

An expression can be used within the body of a tag, but it will only be evaluated if it is not within the body of a tag that is declared to be tagdependent or empty.

4.1.1 Accessing Data

A JSP expression can access any variable declared within one of the four JSP scopes: page, request, session, and application (these were discussed in detail in Chapter 2). By default, a variable is matched against the list of variables defined by searching the page, request, session, and application scopes (in that order), and the result substituted in place of the variable. If the named variable is not found, the null value is used instead. While extremely useful, the default scope searching does introduce one caveat, namely *variable hiding*, in which one variable hides another in a higher scope level. The following list demonstrates how to access different types of variables:

- an attribute (including a JavaBean) named login: ${login}
- an attribute property named username: ${login.username}
- a member named username of an attribute collection: ${login["username"]}

Variables in the JSP EL must follow the naming rules for identifiers in Java; the variable can contain any number of letters, numbers, or underscore characters, but it must begin with a letter or underscore. (Table 4.1 lists the words that are reserved for use within the JSP EL, along with their area of use.) As a result, you cannot use them as identifiers within an expression; doing so will result in a translation-time error. Of these variables, only the last one is not yet officially in the language. As a general rule, you should also be careful to not use any reserved words from the Java programming language. This should help insulate your JSP code from potential future modifications to the EL.

Keyword Type	Keywords
Literals	true false null
Arithmetic Operators	div mod
Relational Operators	eq ne le ge lt gt
Logical Operators	and or not
Collection/Property Test	empty
Unused	instanceof

Table 4.1: The JSP EL's reserved keywords.

To simplify writing expressions, the JSP EL performs automatic type-coercion. The complete rules are detailed in Section 2.8 of the JSP 2.0 specification, but the basics are fairly straightforward. When converting primitive types, such as int and double, the primitive type is boxed, which means they are wrapped in the corresponding *wrapper* class, such as Integer and Double. Boxing simplifies the rules for type coercion, allowing numerical classes to be treated in similar ways. For example, numerical types are converted to strings by calling the appropriate toString method on the boxed type. Likewise, strings can be converted to a numerical type by calling the appropriate valueOf method in the java.lang.String class.

4.1.2   Implicit Objects

Another time-saving feature included within the JSP EL specification is the availability of several implicit objects, which are listed in Table 4.2. These objects simplify the access to HTTP headers, parameters, and cookies, as well as providing direct access to objects in the different scopes. These scope implicit objects can be used to directly access a scoped object, which can prove faster than allowing the JSP container to search through the different scopes for a particular object.

Implicit objects take precedence over identically named objects, which are in one of the four scopes. As a result, you need to be careful not to accidentally use the name of an implicit object as the name of an EL expression variable. Doing so could result in a hard-to-locate run-time bug.

4.1.3   Literal Values

The JSP EL also defines five types of literal values. Literal values are constants with a particular data type and can be used in expressions along with variables. The five literal types are as follows:

- *Boolean:* true and false
- *Integer:* a combination of the numbers 0 through 9
- *Floating Point:* a combination of the numbers 0 through 9, an optional decimal point, a combination of the numbers 0 through 9, and an optional exponent, which uses scientific notation
- *String:* a string of characters enclosed in quotes
- *Null:* null

To differentiate a floating-point literal from an integer literal, a floating-point literal must either have a decimal point, an exponent, or both. Quotes must be escaped—" with \" and ' with \'—within a string literal only if they are of the same type as the enclosing quotes. To demonstrate, 12345 is an integer literal, 12.345E6 is a floating-point literal, and "Invalid Login" is a string literal in double quotes. 'Valid Login' is a string literal in single quotes.

Implicit Object	Description
pageContext	Encapsulates the context for the current JSP page and provides access to the Web application's context object, the session object for the current client, and the current request object.
param	Provides access to request parameters via a Map between a parameter name and associated String value.
paramValues	Provides access to request parameters via a Map between a parameter name and associated String[] values associated with the single parameter name.
header	Provides access to HTTP Headers via a Map between a header name and associated String value.
headerValues	Provides access to HTTP Headers via a Map between a header name and associated String[] values associated with the single header name.
cookie	Provides access to cookies via a Map between a cookie name and a single Cookie object. Only the first Cookie object, which is implementation dependent, is returned when multiple Cookie objects are associated with the same cookie name.
initParam	Provides access to context initialization parameters via a Map between a parameter name and associated String value.
pageScope	Provides access to objects in the *page* scope via a Map between the attribute's name and value.
requestScope	Provides access to objects in the *request* scope via a Map between the attribute's name and value.
sessioncope	Provides access to objects in the *session* scope via a Map between the attribute's name and value.
applicationScope	Provides access to objects in the *application* scope via a Map between the attribute's name and value.

Table 4.2: The JSP EL's implicit objects.

4.1.4 Operators

The JSP EL allows more than just simple access to scoped variables and literals. The EL supports a number of operators, shown in Table 4.3, including support for arithmetic, relational, and logic operators that can be applied to variables and literals. The operators in Table 4.3 are also listed in order of precedence, so *unary negation* has a higher precedence than *multiplication*. Also shown in the table are alternative versions for some of the operators, which can be used in XML documents so entity references are not required.

Operator	Alternative	Description
[ ]		Collection member access
.		Property access
( )		Grouping
-		Unary negation
!	not	Logical not
Empty		Empty test
*		Multiplication
/	div	Division
%	mod	Modulo or division remainder
+		Addition
-		Subtraction
<	lt	Less than
>	gt	Greater than
<=	le	Less than or equal
>=	ge	Greater than or equal
==	eq	Equality
!=	ne	Inequality
&&	and	Logical and
||	or	Logical or
=		Assignment
? :		Conditional operator

Table 4.3: The operators in the JSP EL listed in order of precedence.

JSP EL operations are demonstrated in operators.jsp, which shows different opera-tors acting on integer, floating-point, and Boolean literals. As this example shows, building expressions is simple, and the intuitive results are shown in Figure 4.1. The rest of this chapter will demonstrate other operators and their uses.

Example 4.1 operators.jsp

```
<html>
 <title>Using JSP EL Operators</title>
 <body>
  <h2> Using JSP EL Operators</h2>

  <table border ="2">
   <tr> <td> 13 + 2 = ${13 + 2} </td> </tr>
   <tr> <td> 13 - 2 = ${13 - 2} </td> </tr>
   <tr> <td> 13 * 2 = ${13 * 2} </td> </tr>
   <tr> <td> 13 / 2 = ${13 / 2} </td> </tr>
   <tr> <td> 13 % 2 = ${13 % 2} </td></tr>
```

Using JSP EL Operators

13 + 2 = 15
13 - 2 = 11
13 * 2 = 26
13 / 2 = 6.5
13 % 2 = 1
13.24 + 2 = 15.24
13.24 - 2 = 11.24
13.24 * 2 = 26.48
13.24 / 2 = 6.62
true and false = false
true or false = true
not false = true

Figure 4.1: Using the JSP EL operators.

```
<tr> <td></td> </tr>
<tr> <td> 13.24 + 2 = ${13.24 + 2} </td> </tr>
<tr> <td> 13.24 - 2 = ${13.24 - 2} </td> </tr>
<tr> <td> 13.24 * 2 = ${13.24 * 2} </td> </tr>
<tr> <td> 13.24 / 2 = ${13.24 / 2} </td> </tr>
<tr> <td></td> </tr>
<tr> <td> true and false = ${true && false} </td></tr>
<tr> <td> true or false = ${true || false} </td></tr>
<tr> <td> not false = ${! false} </td></tr>
```

```
  </tr>
  </table>
 </body>
</html>
```

4.2   EL and JavaBeans

Chapter 3 introduced JavaBeans and their application within JSP pages. Before EL was available, JavaBean properties were typically accessed using a JSP expression. However, EL expressions can be used to simplify access to JavaBean properties. For example, you could access the username property of the login JavaBean using a JSP expression:

```
<%= login.getUsername() %>
```

or using an EL expression:

```
${login.username}
```

Using this idea, we can rewrite our login form page from Chapter 3 using EL expressions as in login-bean.jsp. The result, shown in Figure 4.2, is the same as before, but we now have

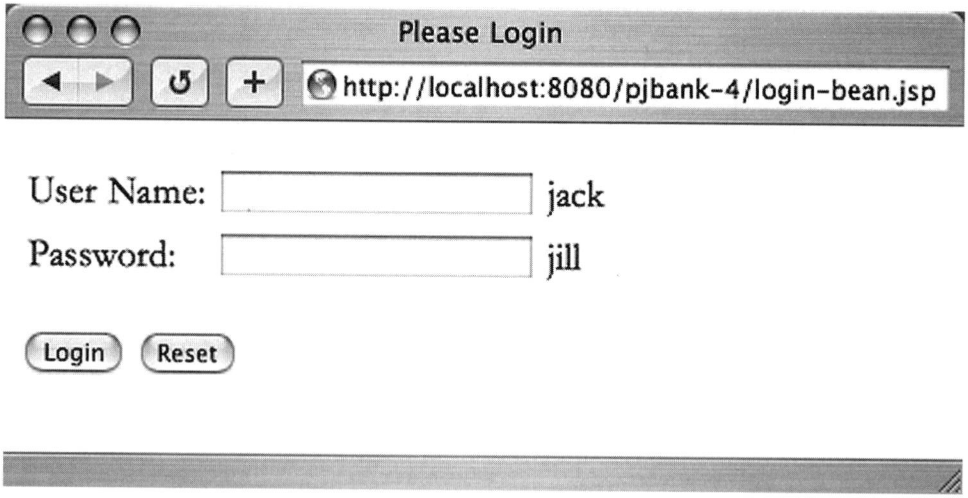

Figure 4.2: Accessing JavaBean properties in a login page using the JSP EL.

no Java code in the entire page. A Web developer, who only knows HTML and JavaScript, can build this page with little extra training.

Example 4.2 login-bean.jsp

```
<jsp:useBean id="login" class="com.pjbank.LoginBean" scope="session"/>
<jsp:setProperty name="login" property="*"/>
<html>
 <title> Please Login </title>
 <body>
  <form method="post">
   <fieldset>
    <legend>Login Information</legend>
    <table>
     <tr>
      <td><label for="username">User Name:</label></td>
      <td><input type="text" name ="username" id="username"></td>
      <td>${login.username}</td>
     </tr>
     <tr>
      <td><label for="password">Password:</label></td>
      <td><input type="password" name ="password" id="password"></td>
      <td>${login.password}</td>
     </tr>
    </table>
    <p/>
    <input type="submit" value="Login">
    <input type="reset">
   </fieldset>
  </form>
 </body>
</html>
```

The simplicity of the property access operator (.) is already evident, but it becomes even more obvious when accessing nested properties. The following example is considerably easier to write and read than the corresponding nested function calls (i.e., cart.getItem().getDescription()).

> ${cart.item.description}

This simpler method is shown in properties.jsp, in which we use the property-access operator to access Servlet properties. This page is displayed in Figure 4.3. For a change of pace, note how the descriptive text is processed as String literals within EL expressions, rather than just placed in situ as template text.

Figure 4.3: Accessing JSP/Servlet properties using the JSP EL.

Example 4.3 properties.jsp

```
<html>
 <title>JSP/Servlet Property Access Using JSP EL </title>
 <body>
  <h2> JSP/Servlet Property Access Using JSP EL</h2>
  <table border ="2">
   <tr>
    <td> ${"Server Information"} </td>
    <td> ${pageContext.servletContext.serverInfo} </td>
   </tr>
   <tr>
    <td> ${"Server Name"} </td>
    <td> ${pageContext.request.serverName} </td>
   </tr>
   <tr>
    <td> ${"Server Port"} </td>
    <td> ${pageContext.request.serverPort} </td>
   </tr>
   <tr>
    <td> ${"Request Protocol"} </td>
```

```
    <td> ${pageContext.request.protocol} </td>
   </tr>
   <tr>
    <td> ${"Session ID"} </td>
    <td> ${pageContext.session.id} </td>
   </tr>
   <tr>
    <td> ${"Session Creation Time"} </td>
    <td> ${pageContext.session.creationTime} </td>
   </tr>
  </table>
 </body>
</html>
```

The JSP EL also allows JavaBean properties to be treated as items in a named collection. As a result, properties can be accessed using the collection member operator ([ ]).

```
     ${login["username"]}
```

This different approach may not seem useful until you remember the rules for type coercion; other data types or even other expressions can be used within the braces, via type coercion to an intermediate String attribute, allowing for dynamic access. This capability is demonstrated in more detail in the next section.

4.3 EL and Collections

Scoped attributes, or variables, can be assigned to any Java object. Perhaps the most useful object types that can now be easily used within a JSP page are Java arrays and classes that implement the java.util.Map and java.util.List interfaces. These collection classes can be accessed within the JSP EL using the collection member access operator. This is demonstrated in headers.jsp, which is shown in Figure 4.4, in which the implicit header object is used to access the HTTP Headers associated with the current client request.

Example 4.4 headers.jsp

```
<html>
 <title> EL HTTP Header Access </title>
 <body>
  <h2> HTTP Header Access Using JSP EL</h2>
  <table border ="2" align="center">
   <tr>
    <td> Connection </td>
    <td> ${header["Connection"]} </td>
   </tr>
```

HTTP Header Access Using JSP EL

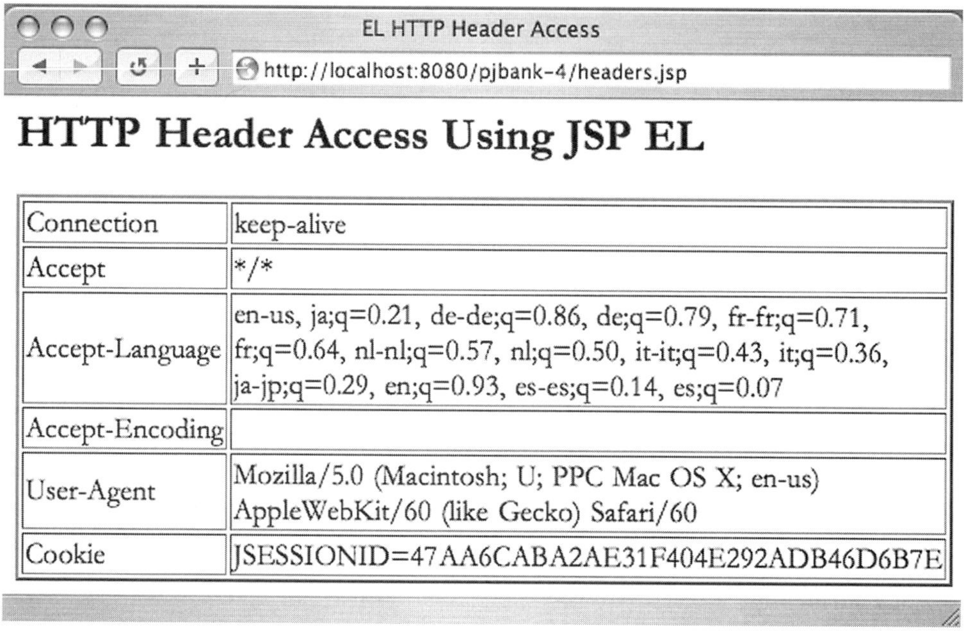

Connection	keep-alive
Accept	*/*
Accept-Language	en-us, ja;q=0.21, de-de;q=0.86, de;q=0.79, fr-fr;q=0.71, fr;q=0.64, nl-nl;q=0.57, nl;q=0.50, it-it;q=0.43, it;q=0.36, ja-jp;q=0.29, en;q=0.93, es-es;q=0.14, es;q=0.07
Accept-Encoding	
User-Agent	Mozilla/5.0 (Macintosh; U; PPC Mac OS X; en-us) AppleWebKit/60 (like Gecko) Safari/60
Cookie	JSESSIONID=47AA6CABA2AE31F404E292ADB46D6B7E

Figure 4.4: HTTP Header names and values displayed using the JSP EL.

```
<tr>
 <td> Accept </td>
 <td> ${header["Accept"]} </td>
</tr>
<tr>
 <td> Accept-Language </td>
 <td> ${header["Accept-Language"]} </td>
</tr>
<tr>
 <td> Accept-Encoding </td>
 <td> ${header["Accept-Encoding"]} </td>
</tr>
<tr>
 <td> User-Agent </td>
 <td> ${header["User-Agent"]} </td>
</tr>
<tr>
 <td> Cookie </td>
 <td> ${header["Cookie"]} </td>
</tr>
</table>
```

```
</body>
</html>
```

The header implicit object is an instance of a class that implements the java.util.Map class. The EL expression header["Cookie"] calls the get method and uses the string "Cookie" as the map key to extract the associated map value, in this case the value of the cookie header. If a key does not exist in the map, the expression evaluates to the null literal, and no exceptions are thrown.

Another, albeit similar, example of extracting collection members is shown in parameters.jsp, but this time we first set several request parameters, then extract them from the HTTP request using the param object. The resulting page, shown in Figure 4.5, displays the request parameters that were entered. Like the header-implicit object, the param object is an instance of a class that implements the java.util.Map class.

Figure 4.5: HTTP request parameter names and values displayed using the JSP EL.

Example 4.5 parameters.jsp

```
<html>
 <title> Parameter Access Using JSP EL</title>
 <body>
  <h2> Parameter Access Using JSP EL</h2>
<%! int counter = 0 ; %>
<%
if(counter == 0) {
  counter++ ;
%>
  <form>
   <fieldset>
    <legend>Enter Information</legend>
    <table>
     <tr>
      <td><label for="username">First Name:</label></td>
      <td><input type="text" name ="First Name"></td>
     </tr>
     <tr>
      <td><label for="username">Last Name:</label></td>
      <td><input type="text" name ="Last Name"></td>
     </tr>
     <tr>
      <td><label for="username">Gender:</label></td>
      <td><input type="text" name ="Gender"></td>
     </tr>
     <tr>
      <td><label for="username">Age:</label></td>
      <td><input type="text" name ="Age"></td>
     </tr>
     <tr>
      <td><label for="username">Address:</label></td>
      <td><input type="text" name ="Address"></td>
     </tr>
    </table>
    <p/><input type="submit" value="Submit">
     <input type="reset">
   </fieldset>
  </form>
<%
 }else{
%>
  <table border ="2">
   <tr>
    <td> First Name </td>
    <td> ${param["First Name"]} </td>
```

```
    </tr>
    <tr>
     <td> Last Name </td>
     <td> ${param["Last Name"]} </td>
    </tr>
    <tr>
     <td> Gender </td>
     <td> ${param["Gender"]} </td>
    </tr>
    <tr>
     <td> Age </td>
     <td> ${param["Age"]} </td>
    </tr>
    <tr>
     <td> Address </td>
     <td> ${param["Address"]} </td>
    </tr>
   </table>
<% } %>
 </body>
</html>
```

The two previous examples (headers.jsp and parameters.jsp) demonstrated the access of members of a Map object, but EL expressions can also work with arrays, including arrays of primitives. The next example, array.jsp, allows the user to select a number between 3 and 10. Depending on the user's selection, which is accessed via a request parameter, the corresponding shape is named, as shown in Figure 4.6.

Example 4.6 array.jsp

```
<%! int count = 0 ;
 String[] shapes = {"Triangle", "Square", "Pentagon", "Hexagon",
    "Heptagon", "Octagon", "Nonagon", "Decagon"} ;
%>

<html>
 <title> Dynamic Array Evaluation </title>
 <script src='scripts/login.js'></script>
 <body>

<% pageContext.setAttribute("shapes", shapes) ;
 if(count == 0) {
  count++ ;
%>
  <form>
   <fieldset>
```

Figure 4.6: Dynamic array evaluation using the JSP EL.

```
    <legend>Enter a number between 3 and 10</legend>
    <table>
     <tr>
      <td><label for="number">Number:</label></td>
      <td><input type="text" name ="number"></td>
     </tr>
    </table>
    <p/><input type="submit" value="Submit"><input type="reset">
   </fieldset>
  </form>
<% } else { %>
  <h2> You Selected a ${shapes[param["number"] - 3]} </h2>
  <hr/>
<% } %>
 </body>
</html>
```

This example demonstrates several interesting points. First, notice how the collection members are nested, following the precedence rules. The number request parameter is extracted before anything else occurs. Second, the request parameter is type coerced to int to participate in an arithmetic operation with an integer literal. Finally, the result of the subtraction is used to extract the appropriate element of the shapes array.

Another important point to take away from this example is the requirement of a JSP declaration and a JSP scriptlet. To put all the necessary functionality within a single JSP page, the counter variable is used to control whether the Hypertext Markup Language (HTML) form or the selected shape is displayed. Second, for the EL expression to access the shape array it must be added to the current page's context. This makes the shapes array visible within the page scope. In the next chapter, these requirements will be removed, allowing this page to be written without any Java code.

List objects are processed in a similar fashion to array objects. For both arrays and lists, if an attempt is made to access a member outside the bounds of the collection, null is returned. Other errors result in an exception being thrown. This list of other errors includes an inability to convert the array indexer to an integer. For example, in shapes[myIndex], if myIndex cannot be converted to an integer so the associated array value can be extracted, an exception is thrown.

4.4 Functions

The first Expression Language to be available to JSP programmers was part of the JSTL. One of the major additions to this earlier EL in the JSP EL is the ability to create and call static functions within an EL expression. This feature allows Java developers to augment the JSP EL and allows Web developers to easily leverage complex functionality without having to add Java constructs directly into a JSP document.

Although this simplifies the life of Web developers, someone has to design and implement the EL function. This process, although straightforward, is rather lengthy, especially when compared to the other features of the JSP EL. First, the function has to be written. As an example of an EL function, Validate.java shows how to write an EL function, which in this case takes a LoginBean as input and returns a String value that informs the user whether a successful login was performed. One important point to remember is that, unlike a JSP document, an EL function class must be compiled by a Java compiler prior to use.

Example 4.7 Validate.java

```
package com.pjbank.functions;

import com.pjbank.LoginBean ;

public class Validate {

  public static String validate(LoginBean lb) {
    try{
      if((lb.getUsername().equals("jack"))&&
        (lb.getPassword().equals("jill")))
        return "Valid Login" ;
```

```
      return "Invalid Login, Please try again." ;
   }catch(NullPointerException ex) { // No login data
      return "Please Login." ;
   }
 }
}
```

The important point to draw from Validate.java is that the method signature indicates that this method is static. The rest of the method signature is encoded in a *Tag Library Descriptor*, or *TLD*, file. These files will not be properly introduced until Chapter 6, but writing a TLD file to describe an EL function is rather straightforward. As seen below in functions.tld, the start of the page is XML that defines the relevant XML namespaces and tag library, or taglib, version. This text can be cut and pasted between different TLD files. For the current discussion, the only relevant text is contained within the function element.

The child elements of the function element provide the requisite information about the function to the JSP container. The name element provides the function name used in an EL expression to call the function. The function-class element directs the JSP container to the function's implementation class. The function-signature element allows the JSP container to verify that the function invocation is syntactically correct.

Example 4.8 functions.tld

```
<?xml version="1.0" encoding="UTF-8" ?>

<taglib xmlns="http://java.sun.com/xml/ns/j2ee"
   xmlns:xsi="http://www.w3.org/2001/XMLSchema-instance"
   xsi:schemaLocation="http://java.sun.com/xml/ns/j2ee web-jsptaglibrary_2_0.xsd"
   version="2.0">

   <tlib-version>1.2</tlib-version>

   <function>
     <description>Validates a User Login attempt</description>
     <name>validate</name>
     <function-class>com.pjbank.functions.Validate</function-class>
     <function-signature>
       java.lang.String validate( com.pjbank.LoginBean )
     </function-signature>
   </function>

</taglib>
```

For the JSP container to map a function call to the appropriate function, a mapping must be established. EL functions use the taglib directive, first described in Chapter 2, to associate a namespace prefix, such as pjbank, with a Universal Resource Indicator (URI). The URI is mapped to the appropriate TLD file in the Web application's deployment descriptor. As an example, the deployment descriptor for the EL function in our example Web application is shown in web.xml.

As was the case with the TLD file, most of the deployment descriptor is standard XML defining the relevant namespaces that are used in web.xml. The important part of this file is the taglib element, in which the taglib-uri element associates a URI with a TLD file, which is specified in the taglib-location element. In this case, functions.tld is located in the WEB-INF subdirectory of the current context.

Example 4.9 web.xml

```
<?xml version="1.0" encoding="ISO-8859-1"?>

<web-app xmlns="http://java.sun.com/xml/ns/j2ee"
  xmlns:xsi="http://www.w3.org/2001/XMLSchema-instance"
  xsi:schemaLocation="http://java.sun.com/xml/ns/j2ee web-app_2_4.xsd"
  version="2.4">

  <taglib>
    <taglib-uri>http://www.pjbank.com/tags</taglib-uri>
    <taglib-location>/WEB-INF/functions.tld</taglib-location>
  </taglib>

</web-app>
```

Now that the function has been defined and compiled and the tag library descriptor and deployment descriptor files created, the function can be used within an EL expression. The validate function is demonstrated in login.jsp. The majority of this JSP document is similar to login-bean.jsp shown earlier in this chapter, with two notable exceptions. First, the taglib directive is used to associate the namespace prefix pjbank with the *http://www.pjbank.com/tags* URI. Because this URI was associated with functions.tld in the deployment descriptor, the JSP container can track down the function's implementation.

The second difference is the function invocation ${pjbank:validate(login)} inside an EL expression. This invocation is easy to follow, as the pjbank prefix defines which validate method should be invoked, and the login JavaBean is passed in as the function's argument. The result of the function call is placed into the JSP output stream and shown in Figure 4.7.

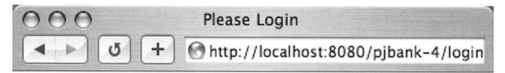

Figure 4.7: The login page showing a successful login attempt.

Example 4.10 login.jsp

```
<%@ page errorPage="exception.jsp" %>
<%@ taglib prefix="pjbank" uri="http://www.pjbank.com/tags" %>

<jsp:useBean id="login" class="com.pjbank.LoginBean" scope="session"/>
<jsp:setProperty name="login" property="*"/>

<html>
<title> Please Login </title>
<script src='scripts/login.js'></script>
<body>
 <h2> ${pjbank:validate(login)} </h2>
 <form>
  <fieldset>
   <legend>Login Information</legend>
   <table>
    <tr>
     <td><label for="username">User Name:</label></td>
     <td><input type="text" name ="username" id="username"></td>
     <td>${login.username}</td>
```

```
    </tr>
    <tr>
     <td><label for="password">Password:</label></td>
     <td><input type="password" name ="password" id="password"></td>
     <td>${login.password}</td>
    </tr>
   </table>
   <p/><input type="submit" value="Login">
    <input type="reset">
   </fieldset>
  </form>
 </body>
</html>
```

Although this function is somewhat contrived for simplicity, it demonstrates how to add more features to the EL easily using functions. For example, the validate function could perform more complicated user validation. Alternatively, functions could be written to provide advanced mathematical functionality, such as trigonometric functions, to EL expressions.

Exercises

1. Write a JSP page that uses EL expressions to create a multiplication table.

2. Write a JSP page that first creates several cookies and then displays them using EL expressions to access the collection. For this problem, you can use a scriptlet to create new cookies using the Cookie class and add them to the response object within a form. The display component of the JSP document should access the cookies via the cookie implicit object.

3. Using the ShoppingCart JavaBean you wrote for Chapter 3, write a JSP that accesses the contents of the shopping cart using EL expressions.

4. Write an EL function that returns the sine of its input, which is assumed to be an angle in degrees.

5. Write a Tag Library Descriptor for your new EL function. Save this file as function.tld.

6. Modify a deployment descriptor to associate a URI with your new EL function TLD file. You can create a fictitious URI for this problem.

7. Write a JSP page that uses your EL function to calculate the sine of several different angles.

chapter **5**

The Standard Tag Library

The last chapter introduced the JavaServer Pages 2.0 Expression Language (EL). The first EL to be made available to JSP developers actually was part of the JSP Standard Tag Library (JSTL) and is a direct ancestor of the JSP 2.0 EL. Together with the new actions defined in the JSTL, EL expressions allowed script-free JSP pages to be written. This made the job of a page developer considerably easier, and it greatly increased the number of people who could be recruited to develop Web applications using JSP technology. In addition, tools such as integrated development environments (IDEs) can capitalize on this simplicity and allow the construction of JSP Web applications in an identical manner to the construction of a Hypertext Markup Language (HTML) page.

This might seem like hyperbole, but tags are an extremely powerful concept and are one of the most important benefits of using JSP over competing technologies. A tag essentially extends the JSP language by encapsulating an action, such as setting a variable or calling a database, within a construct that looks and acts like an HTML tag. To minimize tag incompatibilities, when multiple tags libraries are released that provide similar functionality (and likely tie a developer to a specific application server), the JSP Standard Tag Library was developed.

The rest of this chapter introduces the different tags included in the JSTL. These tags are grouped into four tag libraries: *Core*, *Formatting*, *XML*, and *SQL*. This chapter will discuss the Core tag library in considerable detail because of its simplicity and ubiquity in advanced JSP applications. The other three tag libraries are more complex and are only superficially covered in this chapter.

One of the powerful features of these tags is their ability to cooperate. By nesting tags inside the body of another tag, the tags can implicitly cooperate with each other. This is possible because the inner tags can access the outer tag as an ancestor tag. On the other hand, tags can also cooperate *explicitly* by defining a scoped variable that can be used by subsequent tags in the same JSP page. By default, tags use an attribute named var to define a scoped variable.

The libraries in the JSTL come in two different versions. The first version, EL (which stands for Expression Language), allows EL expressions to be used to specify the value of certain attributes. The second version, RT (which stands for Runtime), only allows run-time expressions, not EL expressions, to specify attribute values. The two libraries are differentiated by the Universal Resource Indicator (URI) used to reference them in a taglib directive. All tags share the same base URI: *http://java.sun.com/jstl/*. The next part of the URI is the tag library's short name: core, fmt, xml, or sql. By default, the URI points to the EL version of the tag library. If the run-time expression version of the library is required, the URI ends in _rt. Thus, in the example below, the first taglib directive associates the c prefix with the EL version of the core tag library, while the second taglib directive associates the fmt prefix with the RT version of the formatting tag library.

```
<%@ taglib uri="http://java.sun.com/jstl/core" prefix="c" %>
<%@ taglib uri="http://java.sun.com/jstl/fmt_rt" prefix="fmt" %>
```

After reading the last chapter, you should clearly favor EL expressions, since they provide greater functionality and are easier to use. However, when using the JSTL with a JSP 2.0 container, you must use the RT version of the JSTL. If you try to use EL expressions, both the JSP 2.0 container and the JSTL will try to handle the EL expression, resulting in an error condition. Until JSP 2.0 containers provide built-in support for JSTL, or a maintenance version of JSTL is made available, the RT version is required.

5.1   Core Tags

The first JSTL tag library contains the core tags, which provide programming support to the JSP developer without the need for JSP declarations or scriptlets. When combined with EL expressions, these tags greatly reduce the need for Java code in JSP pages and, by themselves, make it worth learning the JSTL. This tag library, which is summarized in Table 5.1, can be categorized into four subgroups—general actions, conditional actions, iterator actions, and URL actions—which will be covered in that order.

5.1.1   General Actions

The general action group of core tags consists of four different tags: set, remove, out, and catch, and they operate as you might expect. Briefly, the set tag is used to declare and optionally initialize a scoped variable, the remove tag removes a variable from a specific scope, the out tag writes a scoped variable to the current output stream, and the catch tag provides simple exception-handling support.

Tag Name	Description
set	Define and initialize scoped variable
remove	Remove variable from scope
out	Generate text output
catch	Catch a thrown exception
if	Conditional evaluate tag body based on expression
choose	Select from mutually exclusive conditions based on expression
when	Evaluate body content when expression is true
otherwise	Default body content for choose tag
forEach	Iterate over a collection of objects
forTokens	Iterate over a tokenized string
import	Include external content in current JSP
redirect	Sends HTTP redirect response
url	Dynamically construct URL
param	Encase HTTP request parameters

Table 5.1: The JSTL core tag library.

Of these four, the set tag is probably the one you will use the most. The set tag can either (optionally) declare and initialize a scoped variable or set the value of JavaBean-compliant object or a java.util.Map object using an attribute or the actual body content of the tag itself. The set tag takes five optional attributes that indicate what is being initialized and how. These five attributes are detailed in the following list:

- The value attribute is the expression to be assigned to the target variable or object.
- The target attribute is the object whose property will be set.
- The property attribute specifies the name of the property in the target object to set.
- The var attribute contains the name of the scoped variable to be set.
- The scope attribute indicates to what scope the variable should be assigned; the default value is the page scope.

These five attributes provide a great deal of flexibility in how the set tag can be used. In fact, there are four different ways to use the set tag. First, a scoped variable can be assigned a new value using an attribute:

```
<c:set var="count" value="10" />
```

The previous example set the value of the count variable to 10. If the count variable does not exist, it will be created and placed in the page scope, which is the default value. If no value attribute is present, the default is to use the content of the tag's body to initialize the variable.

```
<c:set var="count">
${count + 1}
</c:set>
```

The preceding example uses an EL expression to increase the value of the count variable by one. Using the body of the set tag is useful when assigning long strings to a variable, something that can prove important when working with databases or XML documents. The properties of a JavaBean-compliant object, such as LoginBean, can be initialized:

```
<c:set target="login" property="username" value="jack"/>
```

This statement sets the username of the LoginBean to jack. This value could also be specified in the body of the tag:

```
<c:set target="login" property="username">
 ${param.username}
</c:set>
```

This previous example demonstrates the username property being set to the value of the username request parameter.

The remove tag is easy to understand, as it simply removes a variable or object from a scope. As a result, the variable or object can no longer be used in EL expression or tags within a JSP page. The remove tag takes two attributes:

- The var attribute specifies the name of the scoped variable to be removed.

- The scope attribute specifies the scope in which the variable is stored.

For example, the remove tag can be used to remove the count variable from the request scope.

```
<c:remove var="count" scope="request" />
```

The out tag writes to the current output stream. Prior to the JSP 2.0 specification, EL expressions could not be used in template text, such as the body of a tag. As a result, a mechanism for writing an EL expression into the output stream was required and was handled by the out tag. In JSP 2.0-compliant containers, however, EL expressions can be placed in template text. Thus, the out tag currently has few, if any, uses. Nevertheless, the out tag has three attributes:

- The value attribute is the expression that should be evaluated and written into the output stream.

- The escapeXml attribute takes a Boolean value, which defaults to true, and indicates whether the <, >, &, ', and " characters are replaced by their corresponding XML entities in the output stream.

- The default attribute specifies a default expression for the tag.

If the value attribute evaluates to null, the default value is evaluated. If it is not specified or is null, the empty string is written. The value can also be specified in the body of the out tag:

```
<c:out>
 ${count + 1}
</c:out>
```

or the value can be specified using the value attribute:

```
<c:out value="${count + 1}" />
```

In both cases, the value of the EL expression is written into the output stream.

The catch tag can be used to catch exceptions so the Web application can gracefully recover. In general, this tag should be used with great care; most application error conditions should be handled by the JSP exception-handling machinery. In some cases, however, the catch tag can simplify the process of creating Web applications.

The catch tag takes only one attribute, var, which names the scoped variable that will hold the exception object that was thrown. Any exceptions thrown from JSP code within the body of the catch tag will get assigned to the var variable and can be handled appropriately. For example, the following example shows how to catch a "Division by zero" exception, which might happen in cases of user input that has not been validated:

```
<c:catch var="ex">
 ${1/0}
</c:catch>
```

After this tag has been processed, the ex variable will be set to the DivisionByZero exception. When combined with the if tag, this provides a simple error-handling mechanism.

5.1.2 Conditional Actions

The next group of tags in the core tag library are the conditional actions, which include the if, choose, when, and otherwise tags. These tags all support conditional programming, in which an application needs to perform different tasks depending on one or more conditional tests. The if tag works by itself to perform a task if a single condition is true, while the other three tags—choose, when, and otherwise—work together to perform multiple tasks, depending on the results of different conditions.

The if tag takes three attributes:

- The test attribute contains an expression that must evaluate to a Boolean. The test condition determines whether the body of the tag is evaluated and written to the current output stream (true) or not (false).

- The var attribute names a scoped variable that will hold the result of the test expression. The variable will be a Boolean type.

- The scope attribute specifies the scope of the variable declared in the var attribute.

Figure 5.1: Displaying a valid log in.

For example, the if tag can be combined with the previous catch tag to process a caught exception:

```
<c:if test="${ex != null}">
 Division by zero attempted.
</c:if>
```

The choose and otherwise tags do not take any attributes, although the when tag takes the test attribute, which is the same as the if tag's test attribute. These three tags work together. When a JSP container processes a choose tag, the body of the first when tag whose test attribute evaluates to true is processed. If none of the test conditions in the when tags inside a choose tag evaluate to true, the body of the otherwise tag is evaluated. For example, validate.jsp uses these three tags to validate a user's attempt to log in, as shown in Figure 5.1.

Example 5.1 validate.jsp

```
<%@ taglib prefix="c" uri="http://java.sun.com/jstl/core_rt" %>

<jsp:useBean id="login" class="com.pjbank.LoginBean" scope="session" />
<jsp:setProperty name="login" property="*" />
<html>
 <body>
```

```
<c:choose>
 <c:when test="${login.valid == true}" >
  <h2>Congratulations, you have been validated</h2>
 </c:when>
 <c:otherwise>
  <h2> <a href="login.jsp">Please try again</a>, invalid login attempt.</h2>
 </c:otherwise>
</c:choose>

<c:remove var="login" />

</body>
</html>
```

If the user enters a valid username and password, which is determined by the valid property of the LoginBean, a welcoming message is displayed. Otherwise, the user is asked to log in again. Notice that at the end of this page, the LoginBean is removed from scope. This is a good demonstration of how the remove tag can prove useful. Because the JavaBean is removed, the user will be forced to log in again, which can be coupled to a user clicking a "log off" button.

One important point about the differences between the when and if tags is that only the first when tag whose test condition is true has its body processed. In contrast to this, the if tag always evaluates its body when its test condition is true. Thus, if multiple conditions may need to be sequentially processed, be sure to use multiple if tags rather than multiple when tags.

5.1.3 Iterator Actions

In addition to conditional processing, the other main programming task often required is loop processing, which is useful for producing HTML tables or iterating over a collection. The core tag library provides two tags that enable looping in JSP pages: forEach and forTokens. The forEach tag iterates over a collection of objects, while the forTokens tag iterates over tokens in a string. As a result of its generality, the forEach tag finds many uses and is very common, especially when accessing EL implicit objects, as shown in headers.jsp.

Example 5.2 headers.jsp

```
<%@ taglib uri="http://java.sun.com/jstl/core_rt" prefix="c" %>

<html>
 <title> Display HTTP Headers </title>
 <body>
```

```
<h2> Display HTTP Headers </h2>
<table border="2">
 <tr> <th> Header Name </th> <th> Header Value </th>
 <c:forEach var="head" items="${header}">
  <tr>
   <td> ${head.key} </td>
   <td> ${head.value} </td>
  </tr>
 </c:forEach>
 </table>
</body>
</html>
```

As shown in Figure 5.2, headers.jsp iterates over the header implicit object, displaying the key (which is the header name) and the value for each header. This example clearly demonstrates the power of combining EL expressions with JSTL tags. In this case, the

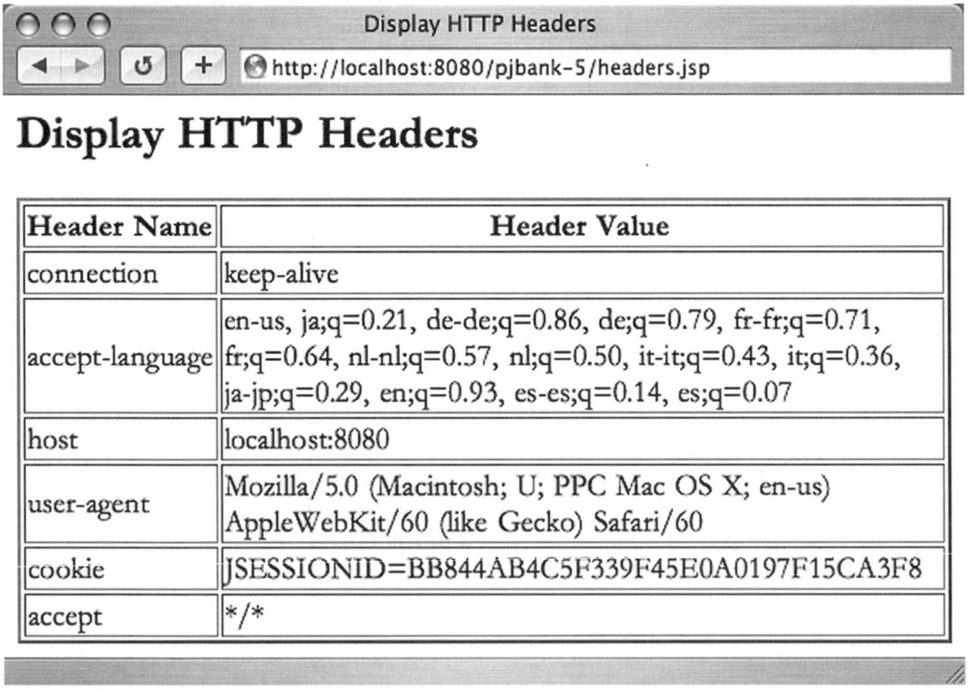

Header Name	Header Value
connection	keep-alive
accept-language	en-us, ja;q=0.21, de-de;q=0.86, de;q=0.79, fr-fr;q=0.71, fr;q=0.64, nl-nl;q=0.57, nl;q=0.50, it-it;q=0.43, it;q=0.36, ja-jp;q=0.29, en;q=0.93, es-es;q=0.14, es;q=0.07
host	localhost:8080
user-agent	Mozilla/5.0 (Macintosh; U; PPC Mac OS X; en-us) AppleWebKit/60 (like Gecko) Safari/60
cookie	JSESSIONID=BB844AB4C5F339F45E0A0197F15CA3F8
accept	*/*

Figure 5.2: Presenting HTTP Headers using JSTL.

header object implements the java.util.Map interface. The iteration variable, which is head in this example, is assigned a new Map entry each time through the loop, and it provides direct access to the key and value for each Map entry.

The forEach tag[1] can easily iterate over a number of different collection classes, including Array objects, a String containing comma-separated value data, or objects that implement the java.util.Collection, the java.util.Iterator, the java.util. Enumeration, or the java.util.Map interfaces. The forEach tag provides all this functionality using only six attributes:

- The var attribute names the exported scoped variable that contains the current item in the iteration.

- The items attribute provides the collection that will be iterated over.

- The varStatus attribute names a scoped variable that contains the status of the iteration.

- The begin attribute specifies the starting index for an iteration.

- The end attribute specifies the ending index for an iteration.

- The step attribute specifies the size of the index increment between iterations.

The forEach tag can also simulate a standard loop, iterating a fixed number of times. For example, the following example displays the numbers 10, 20, 30, etc., up to 100.

```
<c:forEach var="index" begin="10" end="100" step="10">
 ${index}
</c:forEach>
```

The forTokens tag is less complex than the forEach tag, as it iterates over a String containing tokens that are delimited by a specified character. For example, if the keys string contains red:green:blue, the following forTokens tag will iterate over its body content three times, assigning red, green, and blue, respectively, to the key variable.

```
<c:forTokens var="key" items="${keys}" delims=":">
```

5.1.4 URL Actions

The last group of tags in the core tag library provides enhanced support for handling URLs and includes three tags: import, redirect, and url. Each of these tags can have param tags inside their bodies to specify request parameters that should be part of the target URL.

The import tag allows content to be included in the current JSP page, but unlike the include directive or jsp:include action, the import tag allows resources external to the current context to be included. This allows the output from a JSP page to be constructed

---

[1]See section 6.2 of the JSTL specification, available from *http://java.sun.com/products/jsp/jstl*, for complete details.

from resources distributed across the Web. Alternatively, content from external resources can be assigned to a scoped variable. The import tag takes three attributes:

- The url attribute names the URL for the target resource.
- The context attribute names a context for handling relative URL requests.
- The var attribute names the exported scoped variable that will hold the content imported from the external resource.

For example, the following import tag assigns the contents of an external XML file to the scoped variable named funds:

```
<c:import url="/WEB-INF/xml/portfolio.xml" var="funds" />
```

The import tag can also add the content of an external resource to the current output stream, including request parameters (such as username and password) and their values in the HTTP request.

```
<c:import url="validate.jsp">
 <c:param name="username" value="jack">
 <c:param name="password" value="jill">
</c:import>
```

The redirect tag sends an HTTP redirect to the client and takes two attributes: url and context. These attributes function identically to the same attributes in the import tag. The redirect tag can be useful when a user tries to access restricted content without successfully logging in.

```
<c:redirect url="login.jsp" />
```

The url tag can be used to build a URL dynamically, including optional request parameters. If the URL is relative to the current context, the URL can also be rewritten to support session tracking, which is useful when a client does not support cookies. The url tag takes four attributes:

- The value attribute provides the URL to be processed.
- The context attribute names the context to be used when specifying a relative URL.
- The var attribute names the exported scoped variable that contains the processed URL.
- The scope attribute indicates the scope level for the scoped variable named in the var attribute.

The url tag is generally used to dynamically build a URL that can be used in template text with an EL expression. For example, the following example builds a URL that contains the username and password request parameters and assigns it to the check variable.

```
<c:url value="validate.jsp" var="check">
 <c:param name="username" value="jack" />
 <c:param name="password" value="jill" />
```

```
</c:url>
<a href="${check}">Validate<a>
```

5.2 Formatting Tags

The second tag library in the JSTL contains formatting tags, listed in Table 5.2, which simplify supporting localized resources and the internationalization process for JSP applications. The tags in this library support two modes for internationalizing a Web application. The first approach is to provide different versions of JSP pages for each target locale, and it is useful when JSP pages contain a large quantity of localized content. The second approach is to bundle content within a single page that is locale dependent, and this is useful when most of the data on a page is locale independent.

The formatting tag library contains two groups of tags to support localization and internationalization. The first group of tags supports the actual localization of content, and the second group of tags supports the internationalization process.

This first group of tags are primarily responsible for formatting dates, times, and currency in the currently specified locale, which is often just determined from the HTTP headers. These tags include the formatDate, formatNumber, parseDate, parseNumber, timeZone, and setTimeZone tags. Some of these tags take a large number of attributes, which we will not cover here,[2] but their basic usage is straightforward, as is demonstrated in date-time.jsp.

Tag Name	Description
formatDate	Locale-sensitive date/time formatting
formatNumber	Locale-sensitive number/currency/percentage formatting
parseDate	Parse a date/time string
parseNumber	Parse a number/currency/percentage string
timeZone	Specify a time zone for body content
setTimeZone	Specify a time zone for scoped variable
setLocale	Specify a locale for a scoped variable
bundle	Specify a resource bundle for body content
setBundle	Specify a resource bundle for a scoped variable
message	Find a localized message in resource bundle
param	Specify a value for parametric replacement
requestEncoding	Specify HTTP request character encoding

Table 5.2: The JSTL formatting tag library.

---

[2]The formatting action tags are detailed in Chapter 9 of the JSTL specification.

Example 5.3 date-time.jsp

```
<%@ taglib uri="http://java.sun.com/jstl/fmt_rt" prefix="fmt" %>

<jsp:useBean id="today" class="java.util.Date" />

<html>
 <title> Data and Time Formatting </title>
 <body>
  <h2> Data and Time Formatting </h2>
  <hr/>
  <table border="2">
   <tr>
    <td> Both </td>
    <td><fmt:formatDate value="${today}" type="both"
     dateStyle="full" timeStyle="full"/></td>
   <tr>
   <tr>
    <td> Date Only </td>
    <td><fmt:formatDate value="${today}" type="date"
     dateStyle="full" /></td>
   <tr>
   <tr>
    <td> Time Only </td>
    <td><fmt:formatDate value="${today}" type="time"
     timeStyle="full"/></td>
   <tr>
   <tr>
    <td> Custom </td>
    <td><fmt:formatDate value="${today}" type="both"
     pattern="HH:mm, EEEE, dd MMMM yyyy" /></td>
   <tr>
  </table>
 </body>
</html>
```

As is shown in Figure 5.3, the formatDate tag provides support for localized date and time formatting, including custom patterns. Similar functionality is provided for numerical data via the formatNumber tag for currencies, decimal points, and the "thousands separator" character.

The other group of tags supports the process of internationalization, or identifying and bundling locale-specific content. This group of tags includes the setLocale, bundle, setBundle, message, param, and requestEncoding tags. The complete list of attributes and

Data and Time Formatting

Both	Wednesday, April 2, 2003 2:07:35 PM CST
Date Only	Wednesday, April 2, 2003
Time Only	2:07:35 PM CST
Custom	14:07, Wednesday, 02 April 2003

Figure 5.3: Formatting dates and times using JSTL.

usage modes for these tags is lengthy,[3] but as is shown in locale.jsp and displayed in Figure 5.4, their usage is fairly simple.

Example 5.4 locale.jsp

```
<%@ taglib uri="http://java.sun.com/jstl/core_rt" prefix="c" %>
<%@ taglib uri="http://java.sun.com/jstl/fmt_rt" prefix="fmt" %>

<html>
 <title> Internationalization Demonstration </title>
 <body>
  <h2> i18n Demonstration </h2>

  <c:set var="keys" value="Red:Green:Blue" />
  <fmt:setLocale value="en"/>
  <fmt:setBundle basename="com.pjbank.locales.colors" var="enBundle" />
  <fmt:setLocale value="fr"/>
  <fmt:setBundle basename="com.pjbank.locales.colors" var="frBundle" />
  <fmt:setLocale value="de"/>
```

---

[3]For more information on these tags, see Chapter 8 in the JSTL specification.

Figure 5.4: Using the JSTL formatting tags to display color names in English, French, and German.

```
<fmt:setBundle basename="com.pjbank.locales.colors" var="deBundle" />

<table border="2">
  <tr> <th> English </th><th> French </th><th> Deutsch </th> </tr>
  <c:forTokens var="key" items="${keys}" delims=":">
    <tr>
      <td><fmt:message bundle="${enBundle}" key="${key}" /></td>
      <td><fmt:message bundle="${frBundle}" key="${key}" /></td>
      <td><fmt:message bundle="${deBundle}" key="${key}" /></td>
    </tr>
  </c:forTokens>
  </table>
 </body>
</html>
```

This JSP actually demonstrates the power and simplicity afforded by the JSTL and the EL. Notice how the set and forTokens tags cooperate with the message tag to generate the HTML table containing the different locale data. To specify different locales, the setLocale tag is used, while the setBundle tag loads the localized content specified by the basename and current locale into the named scoped variable.

The localized content is specified in the basename attribute using its fully quali-fied name. In this example, the files containing the localized content are stored in the WEB-INF/classes/com/pjbank/locales subdirectory of the current context. The three files are named colors_en, colors_fr, and colors_de, and they provide a mapping between the resource key and its corresponding values, as shown in colors_fr.properties.

Example 5.5 colors_fr.properties

```
Red=rouge
Green=vert
Blue=bleu
```

5.3 XML Tags

Processing XML is a complex task,[4] but the XML tag library, summarized in Table 5.3, within the JSTL provides a number of tags that simplify the parsing, processing, and styling of an XML document. An example is portfolio.xml, which provides information for several different mutual funds in a portfolio.

Example 5.6 portfolio.xml

```
<?xml version="1.0" encoding="UTF-8" ?>

<portfolio>
 <fund>
  <name>Small Cap Fund</name>
  <shares>100</shares>
  <purchase-price>21.25</purchase-price>
  <current-price>23.54</current-price>
 </fund>
 <fund>
  <name>Asia Fund</name>
  <shares>250</shares>
  <purchase-price>13.15</purchase-price>
  <current-price>18.74</current-price>
 </fund>
 <fund>
  <name>Income Fund</name>
  <shares>500</shares>
```

[4]The XML tags are discussed in Chapters 11, 12, and 13 of the JSTL specification.

Tag Name	Description
parse	Parse an XML document
set	Define and initialize scoped variable from XPath expression
out	Generate output from XPath expression
if	Conditional evaluate tag body based on XPath expression
choose	Select from mutually exclusive conditions
when	Evaluate body content when XPath expression is true
otherwise	Default body content for choose tag
forEach	Iterate over body content based on result of XPath expression
transform	Apply XSLT stylesheet to an XML document
param	Encase transformation parameters for transform tag

Table 5.3: The JSTL XML tag library.

```
  <purchase-price>24.50</purchase-price>
  <current-price>27.41</current-price>
 </fund>
</portfolio>
```

To work with this type of structured data, the XML tag library provides tags for loading, parsing, and processing XML data, as shown in portfolio.jsp, which loads the portfolio.xml document using the core tag library's import tag. The parse tag parses the XML data stored in the funds variable and stores the result in the scoped variable named portfolio. The XML tag library has several tags that function in an identical manner to the similarly named tags in the core tag library, including the set, out, if, choose, when, otherwise, and forEach tags.

XML data is accessed using XPath,[5] which is a language that allows XML data to be specified and selected. This is the reason for the new syntax in the value of the XML tag library's forEach tag. The $requestScope: component of the XPath expression instructs the JSP container to look for the portfolio variable in the request scope, which was specified as the scope for the portfolio variable in the parse tag. The /portfolio/* component indicates that all child elements of the portfolio element in the XML data should be selected. Thus, the forEach tag iterates over the three funds in portfolio.xml, displaying the data as shown in Figure 5.5.

Example 5.7 portfolio.jsp

```
<%@ taglib uri="http://java.sun.com/jstl/core_rt" prefix="c" %>
<%@ taglib uri="http://java.sun.com/jstl/xml_rt" prefix="x" %>
```

---

[5] The XPath recommendation is available online at *http://www.w3.org/TR/xpath*.

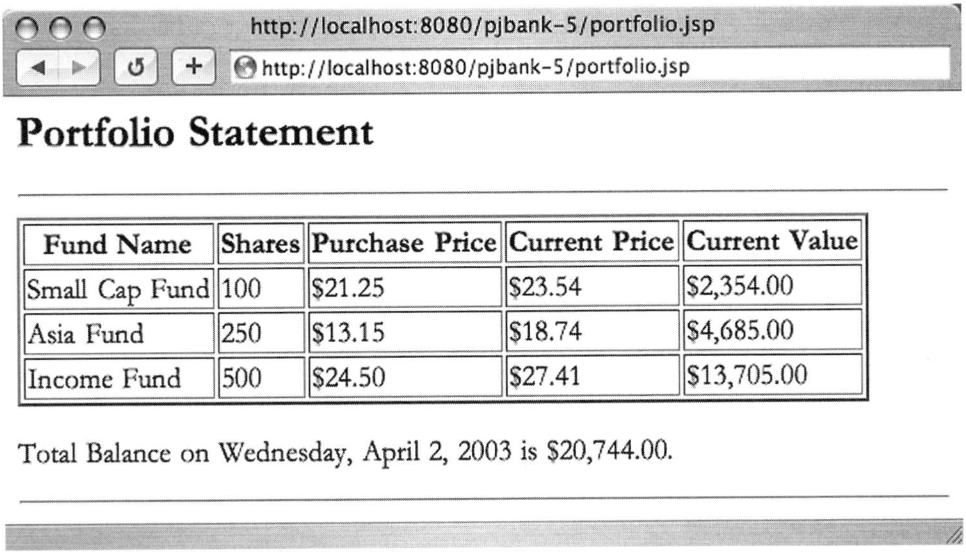
http://localhost:8080/pjbank-5/portfolio.jsp
http://localhost:8080/pjbank-5/portfolio.jsp
Portfolio Statement
Fund Name | Shares | Purchase Price | Current Price | Current Value
Small Cap Fund | 100 | $21.25 | $23.54 | $2,354.00
Asia Fund | 250 | $13.15 | $18.74 | $4,685.00
Income Fund | 500 | $24.50 | $27.41 | $13,705.00
Total Balance on Wednesday, April 2, 2003 is $20,744.00.

Figure 5.5: Presenting formatted XML data.

```
<%@ taglib uri="http://java.sun.com/jstl/fmt_rt" prefix="fmt" %>

<jsp:useBean id="today" class="java.util.Date" />

<html>
 <body>
  <h2> Portfolio Statement </h2>
  <hr/>
  <c:set var="total" value="0" />
  <c:import url="/WEB-INF/xml/portfolio.xml" var="funds" />
  <x:parse xml="${funds}" var="portfolio" scope="request" />
  <table border="2">
   <tr>
    <th>Fund Name</th><th>Shares</th><th>Purchase Price</th>
    <th>Current Price</th><th>Current Value</th>
   </tr>
   <x:forEach var="fund" select="$requestScope:portfolio/portfolio/*">
    <tr>
     <td><x:out select="$fund/name" /></td>
     <c:set var="shares">
      <x:out select="$fund/shares" />
     </c:set>
     <td>${shares}</td>
     <c:set var="pprice">
```

```
   <x:out select="$fund/purchase-price" />
   </c:set>
   <td><fmt:formatNumber value="${pprice}" type="currency"/></td>
   <c:set var="cprice">
    <x:out select="$fund/current-price" />
   </c:set>
   <td><fmt:formatNumber value="${cprice}" type="currency"/></td>
   <td><fmt:formatNumber value="${cprice * shares}" type="currency"/></td>
   </tr>
   <c:set var="total" value="${total + cprice * shares}" />
  </x:forEach>
 </table>
 <p/>
 Total Balance on
 <fmt:formatDate value="${today}" type="date" dateStyle="full" /> is
 <fmt:formatNumber value="${total}" type="currency"/>.<hr/>
</body>
</html>
```

This example also demonstrates the XML tag library's out tag, which selects parts of the XML document using an XPath expression. The $fund/shares expression selects the value of the shares element from the current fund in the iteration. The out tag places the result of the expression directly into the template text, which in this case is the body of a set tag. The end result is to set the value of the shares scoped variable to the value of the current fund's share price.

The formatNumber tag from the formatting tag library is used to output the share price in a locale-specific format. A core tag library set tag accumulates a running total of fund values, which is displayed, along with the current date, using the formatNumber tag after all funds have been iterated over.

5.4 SQL Tags

The last tag library in the JSTL, the SQL tag library, presented in Table 5.4, supports working with databases from within a JSP page. In general, databases should only be accessed from Java Servlets or Enterprise JavaBeans (EJBs). The reasons for this are many, but they can be boiled down to the fact that database connections are expensive both in terms of resources and financial burdens. Furthermore, database operations are often complex and can have potential side effects. Finally, to minimize application dependencies, database-specific code should be encapsulated to as few modules as possible to reduce any code changes that must be made if the underlying database structure is changed. Thus, a general guideline is that only experts, who can ensure that they are performed correctly and maximize database operation throughput, should write database operations.

Tag Name	Description
setDataSource	Define data source
transaction	Define transaction context for enclosed database operations
query	Execute a database SQL query operation
update	Execute a database SQL update operation
param	Specify SQL parameter
dateParam	Specify SQL parameter from Date object

Table 5.4: The JSTL SQL tag library.

With that in mind, some operations are simple enough that database operations from a JSP page are feasible. In addition, sometimes it is easier to prototype a system where the JSP pages handle the database operations, which can be moved to Servlets or EJBs later in the development process. The rest of this section provides a high-level discussion of the SQL tag library,[6] focusing on two JSP examples that insert data into and select data from a database.

The details of connecting a Java application to a database are outside the scope of this book.[7] However, in the interest of completeness, we can quickly cover the basics. To connect to a database, a Java application, such as a JSP page, needs a JDBC driver. The JDBC driver allows a Java application to connect to a database, execute a query, and process any results. A JDBC driver makes a connection to a database using a JDBC URL, which allows the driver to uniquely identify the target database, which can be accessed by a database server running on a different machine. Thus, the class name of the JDBC driver and the exact form of the JDBC URL are required to allow an application to establish a database connection.

Once the connection is established, queries can be executed. A query is written in Structured Query Language (SQL),[8] which is an ANSI standard for interacting with databases. A query can insert new data, modify existing data, delete data, or select data that match certain conditions. A query that selects data is special because it must return that data to the client or, in our case, to a Java application. The selected data is returned to the Java client via a result set, which is like a big table. Rows are iteratively accessed from this result set, allowing a Java application to pull out the data in a simple manner.

For the examples in this section, the database engine used is MySQL, which is a popular open-source database[9] that is also widely documented. A free JDBC driver, Connector/J, can also be downloaded from the MySQL Web site (complete directions are provided in Appendix A). The fully qualified class name for the MySQL driver is com.mysql.jdbc.Driver. To use a different database, the first task is to identify the correct

---

[6]The SQL tag library is detailed in Chapter 10 of the JSTL specification.

[7]A good site for more information is the official JDBC site at *http://java.sun.com/products/jdbc*.

[8]More information on SQL can be found at *http://www.sql.org*.

[9]MySQL can be freely obtained at *http://www.mysql.com*.

Database Name	JDBC Driver Class	Database URL
MySQL	`com.mysql.jdbc.Driver`	`jdbc:mysql://hostname:3306/` `    dbname`
Microsoft Access	`sun.jdbc.odbc.JdbcOdbcDriver`	`jdbc:odbc:DSN`
Oracle 9i	`oracle.jdbc.driver.OracleDriver`	`jdbc:oracle:thin:@hostname:` `    1521:dbname`
IBM DB2 V8.0	`com.ibm.db2.jcc.` `    DB2SimpleDataSource`	`jdbc:db2://hostname:446/` `    dbname`

Microsoft SQL
    Server 2000
	`com.microsoft.jdbc.sqlserver.`
	`    SQLServerDriver`
		`jdbc:microsoft:sqlserver://`
		`    hostname:1433;databasename=`
		`    dbname`

PostgreSQL	`org.postgresql.Driver`	`jdbc:postgresql://hostname:5432/` `    dbname`

Table 5.5: Database-specific JDBC connection information. Note that "hostname" should be replaced by the name of the server running the database (for example, `localhost`) and "dbname" stands for the database name (for example, `pjbank`). DSN stands for data source name, which is the registered name for the ODBC datasource.

JDBC driver. For example, the JDBC-ODBC bridge driver is `sun.jdbc.odbc.JdbcOdbcDriver`. To make a database connection, the JDBC driver requires a JDBC URL to specify the location of the target database. For the MySQL database, the basic URL is `jdbc:mysql://` `localhost/dbname`, where dbname stands for database name. The last two components to make a connection are a username and the appropriate password.

Another possibility would be to use an ODBC-accessible database, such as Microsoft Access, which can be accessed using the JDBC-ODBC bridge driver. This JDBC driver is automatically part of the Java Virtual Machine (JVM) and, as a result, does not need to be explicitly added to a Web application. In addition, other databases such as Oracle's database system, Microsoft's SQL Server, and IBM's DB2 can be used with an appropriate JDBC driver. To simplify the migration of the example code to these alternate databases, Table 5.5 provides the relevant details, including the JDBC driver class name and appropriate JDBC URL for several other databases. This table, however, is merely a guide and is not meant to replace the documentation that comes with your database.

With this background in place, we can now turn to the JSP aspects of our two examples. The first example, `update.jsp`, parses data from the `portfolio.xml` document and inserts it into a database. This example uses three SQL tags: `setDataSource`, which sets up the database connection; `update`, which creates a SQL update statement to send to the database; and `param`, which is used to specify parameters for the SQL statement. In this case, we are using an SQL INSERT statement. As we iterate over the different funds in the portfolio, we create a new INSERT statement, inserting the fund details into the appropriate sections of the SQL INSERT statement with the SQL param tags. The data flow for this example is shown in Figure 5.6.

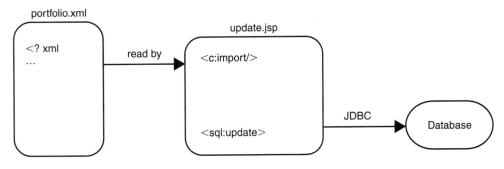

Figure 5.6: The data flow for the SQL UPDATE JSTL example.

Example 5.8 update.jsp

```
<%@ taglib uri="http://java.sun.com/jstl/core_rt" prefix="c" %>
<%@ taglib uri="http://java.sun.com/jstl/xml_rt" prefix="x" %>
<%@ taglib uri="http://java.sun.com/jstl/sql_rt" prefix="sql" %>

<sql:setDataSource driver="com.mysql.jdbc.Driver"
 url="jdbc:mysql://localhost/pjbank"
 user="jack" password="jill"/>

<html>
 <body>
  <h2> Inserting Portfolio into the Database </h2>
  <hr/>
  <c:set var="total" value="0" />
  <c:import url="/WEB-INF/xml/portfolio.xml" var="funds" />
  <x:parse xml="${funds}" var="portfolio" scope="request" />
  <x:forEach var="fund" select="$requestScope:portfolio/portfolio/*">

   <sql:update>
   INSERT INTO PORTFOLIO VALUES(?, ?, ?, ?)
   <sql:param><x:out select="$fund/name" /></sql:param>
   <sql:param><x:out select="$fund/shares" /></sql:param>
   <sql:param><x:out select="$fund/purchase-price" /></sql:param>
   <sql:param><x:out select="$fund/current-price" /></sql:param>
   </sql:update>
   Inserted <x:out select="$fund/name" /> into the database.<br/>

  </x:forEach>
 </body>
</html>
```

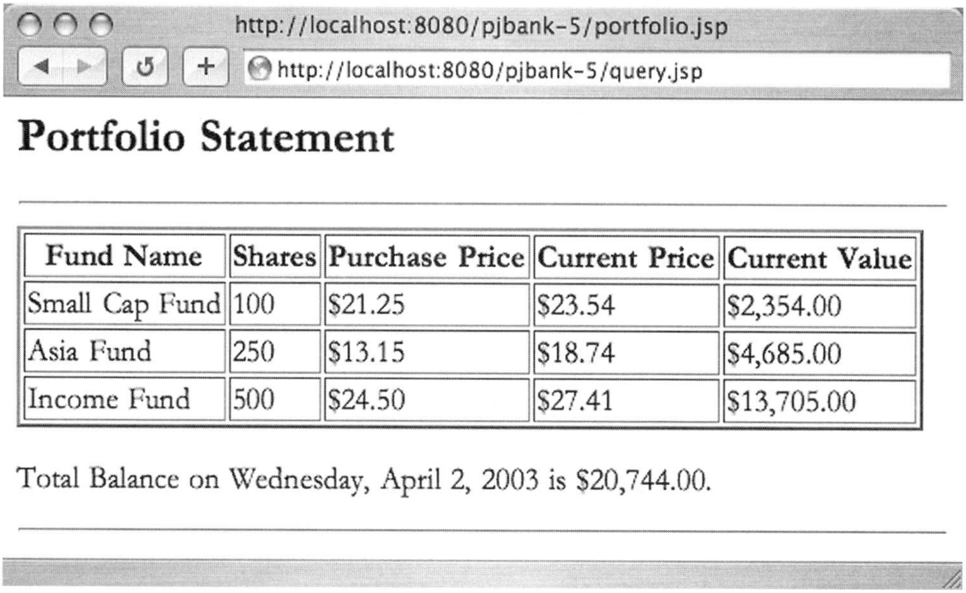

○ ○ ○   http://localhost:8080/pjbank-5/portfolio.jsp

◄ ►   ↻   +   ⊙ http://localhost:8080/pjbank-5/query.jsp

Portfolio Statement

Fund Name	Shares	Purchase Price	Current Price	Current Value
Small Cap Fund	100	$21.25	$23.54	$2,354.00
Asia Fund	250	$13.15	$18.74	$4,685.00
Income Fund	500	$24.50	$27.41	$13,705.00

Total Balance on Wednesday, April 2, 2003 is $20,744.00.

Figure 5.7: Displaying formatted database data.

The setDataSource tag shown in update.jsp contains explicit connection parameters. In general, this is to be discouraged due to the potential for a security breach. This approach is useful for training purposes, however, as it simplifies the complexities of database programming. The recommended approach for using the setDataSource tag is to use a JDBC DataSource that has been registered with a Java Naming and Directory Interface (JNDI) server.

Once the data has been added to the database, we can now query the database to dynamically generate an HTML page, as shown in query.jsp. This example selects all funds from the portfolio database table using the SQL query tag. The query result, which is accessed from a java.sql.ResultSet object, is added to the funds scoped variable, which can be used in a forEach tag to iterate over the individual items in the ResultSet. Using the data for each row in the ResultSet, the fund data is displayed in an HTML table, which is shown in Figure 5.7.

Example 5.9 query.jsp

```
<%@ taglib uri="http://java.sun.com/jstl/core_rt" prefix="c" %>
<%@ taglib uri="http://java.sun.com/jstl/fmt_rt" prefix="fmt" %>
<%@ taglib uri="http://java.sun.com/jstl/sql_rt" prefix="sql" %>

<jsp:useBean id="today" class="java.util.Date" />
```

```
<sql:setDataSource driver="com.mysql.jdbc.Driver"
 url="jdbc:mysql://localhost/pjbank"
 user="jack" password="jill"/>

<html>
 <body>
  <h2> Portfolio Statement </h2>
  <hr/>
  <c:set var="total" value="0" />
  <sql:query var="funds">
   SELECT * FROM portfolio
  </sql:query>
  <table border="2">
   <tr>
    <th>Fund Name</th><th>Shares</th><th>Purchase Price</th>
    <th>Current Price</th><th>Current Value</th>
   </tr>
   <c:forEach var="fund" begin="0" items="${funds.rows}">
    <tr>
     <td>${fund.name}</td>
     <c:set var="shares" value="${fund.shares}" />
     <td>${shares}</td>
     <c:set var="pprice" value="${fund['pprice']}" />
     <td><fmt:formatNumber value="${pprice}" type="currency"/></td>
     <c:set var="cprice" value="${fund['cprice']}" />
     <td><fmt:formatNumber value="${cprice}" type="currency"/></td>
     <td><fmt:formatNumber value="${cprice * shares}" type="currency"/></td>
    </tr>
    <c:set var="total" value="${total + cprice * shares}" />
   </c:forEach>
  </table>
  <p/>
  Total Balance on
  <fmt:formatDate value="${today}" type="date" dateStyle="full" /> is
  <fmt:formatNumber value="${total}" type="currency"/>. <hr/>
 </body>
</html>
```

One final caveat in regard to extracting data from a database must be mentioned. Databases store data using specific data types. In the previous example, the currency data had to be stored in floating-point format. In reality this would not be appropriate because floating-point data types are not suitable for currencies due to their lack of precision for decimal data. Yet if we stored the currency data in integer format, without extra conversions, the JSP tags would pull the data out and truncate the decimal component. This is still another example of why experts should be brought in to handle database operations.

Exercises

1. Name and describe the four tag libraries in the JSTL.

2. Show two different ways to use a JSTL tag to set the value of a variable named count to the value 10.

3. Write a JSP page that uses a form to input a number; then, using only the core conditional tags and EL expressions, write a message that specifies whether the number is even or odd.

4. Write a JSP page that uses the forEach tag to display all cookies.

5. Using JSTL tags and EL expressions, write a JSP page that displays all items in the ShoppingCartBean you wrote in Chapter 3.

chapter **6**

Custom Actions

In the last two chapters, the foundations for building Java-free JSP pages were introduced, namely the JSP Expression Language (EL) and the JSP Standard Tag Library (JSTL). Together, these greatly reduce the need for scriptlets and expressions within a JSP page. One final piece still needs to be discussed, however: how to write custom actions or tags. Custom tags allow JSP developers to simplify complex tasks, and they form the basis for how the JSTL is actually implemented.

The ability to create custom actions has been around since version 1.2 of the JSP specification, and it provides great power to JSP developers. As is generally the case, this power must be used wisely; custom actions introduce new language constructs, which can introduce dependencies that complicate application development, deployment, and maintenance. This concern was one of the primary drivers behind the development of the JSTL, which should always be used in lieu of custom actions wherever possible. The rest of this chapter provides an overview of custom actions, before introducing and demonstrating the different methods that can be used to create them.

6.1 Tag Overview

As you probably gleaned from the last chapter, custom actions can provide powerful functionality in a flexible mechanism. The actions introduced in the JSTL provide useful models for developing your own custom actions. Custom actions can be empty or they can have a body. They can also take attributes and cooperate, either implicitly when nested or explicitly through scoped attributes.

A *tag handler* is a Java class that either implements a specific interface or extends a specific base class and provides the functionality of a custom action. Originally,

117

developing custom actions was a complicated process. One of the new concepts introduced in the JSP 2.0 specification, however, is a simpler tag interface and the ability to develop custom actions using tag files, which greatly simplify the development of simple custom actions. To differentiate the two approaches, tags built using the new approach are called *simple tags*, while tags built using the original approach are called *classic tags*.

One or more custom actions are actually deployed by being bundled together into a tag library. The details of a tag library are provided by the Tag Library Descriptor, or TLD file. This file is an XML document that, among other things, maps a tag name to the appropriate tag handler class. A TLD file can also provide information about the names and types of any attributes for a custom action, as well as information about any scripting variables a tag introduces to a JSP application. With the release of the JSP 2.0 specification, TLD files are written using XML Schema Definition (XSD), which is more powerful than the original Document Type Definition (DTD) used in earlier JSP specifications.

As was demonstrated in Chapter 5, custom tags are introduced into a JSP page using the taglib directive, which maps a prefix to a Universal Resource Indicator (URI) that uniquely identifies a tag library. The mapping between a tag library URI and the relevant TLD file can be provided in the Web application's deployment descriptor, which is the web.xml file. The rest of this section provides more detail on the different types of tag handlers and a more detailed introduction to TLD files.

6.1.1 Tag Handlers

A tag handler provides the actual implementation for a custom action. Two types of tag handlers can be used: a simple tag handler or a classic, or standard, tag handler. The simple tag handler can be used to create custom actions that will be used only in JSP pages that do not contain scriptlets or expressions. Classic tag handlers, on the other hand, do not have this restriction and can be used in a more generic fashion.

Simple tags can be implemented using either a tag handler Java class or a tag file written in JSP. Determining which approach to use when creating simple tags is straightforward. If the tag is primarily focused on the presentation of information or relies solely on other tags, such as those in the JSTL, tag files are a good choice. Due to their power and simplicity, the bulk of this chapter will focus on tag files. On the other hand, more complicated tasks that require Java processing must use a tag handler class.

Simple tag handlers have a basic lifecycle. When needed, the simple tag handler class is instantiated, used, and discarded. Subsequent uses of a simple tag repeat the process, as simple tags are not cached. The body, if present, of a simple tag is translated into a JSP fragment that can be processed repeatedly as needed. Simple tags also do not rely on the Servlet APIs, so in the future they could be used with other technologies. Simple tag handlers can be created by implementing the SimpleTag interface or by extending the SimpleTagSupport class.

In contrast, classic tag handlers are always implemented as a Java class. This class either implements the Tag, IterationTag, or BodyTag interface, or it extends the

TagSupport or BodyTagSupport classes. Classic tag handlers can be reused and provide more fine-grained control over the behavior of a tag handler. The three interfaces provide increasingly greater levels of functionality:

- The Tag interface provides the basic functionality necessary for a tag handler, including methods for initializing attributes and processing at the start and end of a tag handler's invocation, via the doStartTag and doEndTag methods.

- The IterationTag interface extends the Tag interface to provide support for multiple invocations, or iterations, of a tag using the doAfterTag method.

- The BodyTag interface extends the IterationTag interface to provide support for processing a tag's body content, providing the doInitBody method and an encapsulation of the tag's body in a BodyContent object.

Following the JSP specification, tag handlers can be loosely categorized into several groups that can help in determining how to best implement a tag handler. The groups are as follows.

- *Plain actions* simply do something, the details of which might depend on the value of an attribute. The remove and import tags in the core JSTL tag library are good examples. A plain action needs only to implement the doStartTag method in the Tag interface or, for a simple tag handler, the doTag method.

- *Plain actions with a body* do something that can include passing the body of the tag to the output stream. This group of actions can use the doStartTag and doEndTag methods for a classic tag handler, while simple tags use the doTag method and can access the tag's body via a JSP Fragment.

- *Conditional actions* optionally process the body content of the tag depending on some condition. Classic tag handlers can provide this functionality via the return value of the doStartTag method. Simple tag handlers can provide this functionality by conditionally accessing the JSP Fragment that contains the body's content in the doTag method.

- *Iteration actions* process their body multiple times. Classic tag handlers must use the doAfterBody method in the IterationTag interface. Simple tag handlers place the iteration logic in the doTag method.

- *Actions that process their body*, beyond simple output or iteration, use either a BodyContent object to access a classic tag handler's body content or a JSP Fragment for a simple tag handler. In both cases, the actual body content can be reinterpreted and manipulated.

- *Cooperating actions* can share data via scoped variables or via access to parent, or ancestor, tags. This functionality is supported by both classic and simple tag handlers.

6.1.2   Tag Library Descriptors

The TLD file is an XML document that provides a mapping between a taglib URI and the actual tag handler implementations. These TLD files are also used for EL functions, as described in Chapter 4. As of the JSP 2.0 specification, TLD files are written to conform to an XSD document, which is available at *http://java.sun.com/xml/ns/j2ee/ web-jsptaglibrary_2_0.xsd*. All TLD files should have a *.tld* extension and, when deployed as part of a Web application, they should be located inside the application's WEB-INF directory or one of its subdirectories, other than the lib or classes subdirectories. When deployed inside a Java Archive (JAR) file, the TLD file must be located inside the META-INF directory or one of its subdirectories.

A TLD file contains elements that provide information regarding the tag library as a whole, as well as information about individual tag handlers. Individual tag handlers are described using tag elements. These elements have child elements, including the following:

- The name element provides a unique name for this action.

- The tag-class element provides the fully qualified name for the class that provides the tag handler's implementation class.

- The body-content element indicates the content type of the tag's body, which can be empty, JSP, scriptless, or tagdependent.

- The attribute element provides information on the tag's attributes, which has name and type child elements.

To demonstrate, demo.tld is a fictitious TLD file that contains three tags: tagA, tagB, and tagC. The tagA tag has an empty body and takes no attributes. The tagB tag takes a single string attribute named attributeB1. Finally, the tagC tag takes two attributes, a string attribute named attributeC1 and an integer attribute named attributeC2, and it has a JSP body content.

Example 6.1 demo.tld

```
<taglib xmlns="http://java.sun.com/xml/ns/j2ee"
 xmlns:xsi="http://www.w3.org/2001/XMLSchema-instance"
 xsi:schemaLocation="http://java.sun.com/xml/ns/j2ee/web-jsptaglibrary_2_0.xsd"
version="2.0">

<tlib-version>1.2</tlib-version>
<jsp-version>1.2</jsp-version>
<short-name>pjbank</short-name>
<uri>pjbank-tag</uri>

<tag>
 <name>tagA</name>
 <tag-class>com.pjbank.tags.TagA</tag-class>
```

```
   <body-content>empty</body-content>
  </tag>
  <tag>
   <name>tagB</name>
   <tag-class>com.pjbank.tags.TagB</tag-class>
   <body-content>empty</body-content>
   <attribute>
    <name>attributeB1</name>
    <type>java.lang.String</type>
   </attribute>
  </tag>
  <tag>
   <name>tagC</name>
   <tag-class>com.pjbank.tags.TagC</tag-class>
   <body-content>JSP</body-content>
   <attribute>
    <name>attributeC1</name>
    <type>java.lang.String</type>
   </attribute>
   <attribute>
    <name>attributeC2</name>
    <type>java.lang.Integer</type>
   </attribute>
  </tag>
</taglib>
```

6.2 Tag Files

The previous section discussed some of the finer points about writing tag handler implementations. These details are rather lengthy, which prohibits many developers from taking
advantage of the JSP Tag Extension API to develop custom actions. To simplify the process
and allow a wider range of developers to build custom actions, the JSP 2.0 specification
introduced the concept of tag files.

A *tag file* allows a developer to build a custom action using only JSP syntax. Tag files
must have either the *.tag* or *.tagx* extension, with the latter extension reserved for tag files
written using XML syntax. Tag files can be composed of other tag files, in which case the
tag fragment files are recommended to use the *.tagf* file extension.

When deployed as part of a Web application, tag files should be placed in the application's WEB-INF/tags directory or one of its subdirectories. If placed anywhere else, a
tag file is treated as content to be served by the JSP container. On the other hand, when
deployed as part of a JAR file, the tag files must be located in the META-INF/tags directory.
If tags are bundled in a JAR file, a TLD file is required. Otherwise a TLD file is not required,
but it can be used.

Tag files are similar to regular JSP files in many respects. The primary differences are in the JSP directives and standard actions that can be used in a tag file. First, a tag file cannot use the page directive because it is not a JSP page. Instead, tag files use the tag directive, which can only be used in a tag file. Tag files also have two other directives—the attribute and variable directives—that can only be used in tag files. In addition, tag files can use the taglib and include directives. There are also two additional standard actions—jsp:invoke and jsp:doBody—that can only be used inside a tag file.

These directives and standard actions will be detailed later in this section when they are introduced. To demonstrate how easy it is to author a tag file, we can take the welcome JSP page for our PJ Bank Web application and convert it to use tag files. First, we will convert the header JSP page to a tag file. To make things simple to start, the Web page's HTML title element will be hardcoded. The result is shown in header.tag, which is placed inside the WEB-INF/tags directory.

Example 6.2 WEB-INF/tags/header.tag

```
<html>
<head>
 <script src='scripts/login.js'></script>
 <link rel="stylesheet" type="text/css" href="style/pjbank.css"/>
 <title>Welcome to PJ Bank!</title>
</head>

<body>
<img src="images/banner.jpg" width="100%" alt="PersistentJava Bank Banner Image"/>

<hr/>
```

To use this tag file within our welcome page, we first use the taglib directive to map the tag file location to a prefix, then call our new custom action, as shown in the following code example.

```
<%@ taglib prefix="pjbank" tagdir="/WEB-INF/tags" %>

<pjbank:header/>
```

Clearly, this simple example does not do anything overly complicated, but that is the point: Creating custom actions using tag files is not complicated. Although this example did not use it, the tag directive provides information to the JSP container about the tag file in an identical manner as the page directive does. As with the page directive, a tag file can have more than one tag directive, but only the import attribute can be used more than once. Multiple uses of an attribute, other than the import attribute, or the use of unrecognized attributes or values results in a fatal translation error.

The `tag` directive takes the following 11 attributes, all of which are optional:

- The `display-name` attribute provides a short name that can be used by development tools. It defaults to the name of the tag file.

- The `body-content` attribute details the content type of the tag body. Must be either empty, `tagdependent`, or `scriptless`. It defaults to `scriptless`.

- The `dynamic-attributes` attribute indicates whether this tag file supports attributes with dynamic names, which, if it does, allows a tag to be written that supports an arbitrary number of attributes that follow a common naming scheme. It defaults to `false`.

- The `small-icon` attribute provides the path to an image that can be used by JSP development tools as a small icon for this tag file.

- The `large-icon` attribute provides the path to an image that can be used by JSP development tools as a large icon for this tag file.

- The `description` attribute provides an arbitrary string that describes the tag.

- The `example` attribute provides an arbitrary string the gives a description of an example use for the tag.

- The `language` attribute is identical to the page directive's language attribute.

- The `import` attribute is identical to the page directive's `import` attribute.

- The `pageEncoding` attribute is identical to the page directive's `pageEncoding` attribute.

- The `IsELIgnored` attribute is identical to the page directive's `isELIgnored` attribute.

6.2.1 Processing Attributes in a Tag File

The previous `header.tag` example tag file was rather simplistic. To create a custom action that provides all the functionality of our original header JSP Fragment, we must be able to pass in the Web page's title dynamically. To accomplish this, the header custom action needs to take an attribute that will hold the desired title string.

```
<pjbank:header title="Welcome to PJ Bank" />
```

The required modifications to the header tag files are minor. First we declare an attribute using the `attribute` directive, which provides the name of the attribute. The value of the attribute is accessed using an EL expression. Otherwise, as is shown in `headers.tag`, everything else stays the same.

Example 6.3 headers.tag

```
<%@ attribute name="title" %>

<html>
```

```
<head>
 <script src='scripts/login.js'></script>
 <link rel="stylesheet" type="text/css" href="style/pjbank.css"/>
 <title>${title}</title>
</head>

<body>
<img src="images/banner.jpg" width="100%" alt="PersistentJava Bank Banner Image"/>

<hr/>
```

The attribute directive allows a developer to declare attributes for a custom action defined in a tag file in an identical format as the attribute element in a TLD file. The attribute directive has six attributes:

- name is the only required attribute and provides a unique name for the attribute being declared.

- required specifies whether the attribute is optional or required. It defaults to false, which means the attribute is optional.

- fragment indicates whether the attribute's value is a fragment that should be handled by the tag handler. It defaults to false, which means the attribute does not contain a fragment.

- rtexprvalue indicates whether the value of the attribute can be dynamically calculated at run-time by a scriptlet expression. The default value is false, which means scriptlet expressions cannot be used.

- type is the run-time type for the attribute's value. Primitive types cannot be used.

- description provides a description for the attribute.

As a developer, you have a great deal of flexibility in naming attributes. Names, however, should be carefully selected to minimize confusion. A good guide to attribute naming is the JSTL, where standard names such as var and value simplify the task of a tag developer when using new tags.

Tag handlers can take three different types of attributes: *simple*, *fragment*, and *dynamic*. The first type is a simple attribute, which is what was demonstrated in the previous example with the title attribute. The JSP container evaluates simple attributes before the tag handler receives them. Thus, a simple attribute can be set using a String constant, as in the title attribute, or using an expression.

The second type of attribute is the fragment attribute, which is a slice of JSP code that is passed by the JSP container directly to the tag handler for evaluation. The JSP fragment can be processed repeatedly as needed by the tag handler to generate the desired content. Fragment attributes are defined using the jsp:attribute standard action, which can only contain template text and standard and custom JSP actions, not scripting elements.

The last type of attribute is dynamic attributes, which are not defined during the development of the tag. Dynamic attributes are used when a tag will need to uniformly process an arbitrary number of attributes, whose exact name is not known until run-time. For example, this can be used to create a tag that adds together all attributes that follow the naming scheme, value1, value2, ..., valueN.

```
<myTags:Add value1="1" value2="2" ... value100="100" />
```

The actual tag handler that provides the implementation for the tag must accept an arbitrary number of arguments, as long as they follow the indicated naming scheme.

6.2.2 Processing a Tag Body

In addition to an attribute, a tag also can have body content. For example, we can create a footer custom action that displays standard footer information as well as custom content that varies between pages. In our welcome page, we might call the footer tag with copyright information.

```
<pjbank:footer>
&copy; PJBank, 2002
</pjbank:footer>
```

This body content is processed using the doBody standard action, as shown in footer.tag. Other important points to glean from this tag file are the use of the JSTL formatDate custom action as well as the use of the java.util.Date JavaBean. Notice that we did not need to explicitly initialize the Date JavaBean to the current date. This is done automatically during the instantiation of a Date object. The HTML text is written to the JSP output stream, and the doBody standard action is replaced with the value of the footer tag's body content.

Example 6.4 footer.tag

```
<%@ taglib prefix="fmt" uri="http://java.sun.com/jstl/fmt_rt" %>

<jsp:useBean id="today" class="java.util.Date" />

<hr/>
</body>
<address>
<fmt:formatDate value="${today}" type="both" dateStyle="full" timeStyle="full"/>
<br/>
<jsp:doBody/>
</address>
</html>
```

The jsp:doBody action operates on a JSP fragment that contains the body of the originating tag. This standard action can only be used in tag files and will cause a translation error if used anywhere else. The jsp:doBody action can only have white space or jsp:param actions as its body content. This action takes three attributes:

- The var attribute is optional and provides the name of a String object that can store the result of the JSP fragment. It cannot be used in conjunction with the varReader attribute.

- The varReader attribute is an optional attribute that provides the name of a Reader object that can store the result of the JSP fragment. It cannot be used in conjunction with the var attribute.

- The scope attribute specifies the scope level for the resulting variable and can either be page, request, session, or application. This attribute can only occur in conjunction with either the var or varReader attribute and defaults to page.

The body of a simple tag can be dynamically processed, in addition to the static content processed in the footer tag. A good example of a case where this might prove useful is the left-banner JSP page, in which different content is displayed depending on whether a user has been validated or not. The new left-banner.jsp uses the valid tag and two attribute standard actions, which were discussed in Chapter 2, to pass JSP fragments to the tag file. The jsp:attribute standard action allows multiple fragments to be passed into a tag file, with each fragment differentiated by a unique name.

Example 6.5 left-banner.jsp

```
<%@ taglib prefix="pjbank" tagdir="/WEB-INF/tags" %>

<jsp:useBean id="login" class="com.pjbank.LoginBean" scope="session" />
<jsp:setProperty name="login" property="*" />

<table class="border">

<pjbank:valid>
<jsp:attribute name="good">
  <tr><td>
   <font class="start">A</font>
   <font class="rest">ccess Account</font>
  </td></tr>
</jsp:attribute>
<jsp:attribute name="bad">
  <tr><td>
   <a href="login.jsp">
   <font class="start">L</font>
   <font class="rest">ogin</font>
   </a>
```

```
  </td></tr>
</jsp:attribute>
</pjbank:valid>
</table>
```

The valid tag is fairly simple in that it first declares the two attributes for the tag using the attribute directive. Because these two attributes are fragments, and not normal attributes, the fragment attribute is set to true. The JSTL core tag library's conditional tags are used to test whether the login is valid. Depending on this test, one of the JSP fragments is invoked using the jsp:invoke standard action.

Example 6.6 valid.tag

```
<%@ taglib prefix="c" uri="http://java.sun.com/jstl/core" %>

<%@ attribute name="good" fragment="true" %>
<%@ attribute name="bad" fragment="true" %>

<c:choose>
 <c:when test="${login.valid == true}" >
  <jsp:invoke fragment="good" />
 </c:when>
 <c:otherwise>
  <jsp:invoke fragment="bad" />
 </c:otherwise>
</c:choose>
```

The jsp:invoke standard action is used in tag files, in a similar manner as the jsp:doBody standard action, to invoke a JSP fragment. Using this action outside of a tag file results in a translation error. This action takes four attributes:

- The fragment attribute provides the name of the fragment that should be invoked.

- The var attribute is optional and provides the name of a String object that can store the result of the JSP fragment. It cannot be used in conjunction with the varReader attribute.

- The varReader attribute is an optional attribute that provides the name of a Reader object that can store the result of the JSP fragment. It cannot be used in conjunction with the var attribute.

- The scope attribute specifies the scope level for the resulting variable and can either be page, request, session, or application. This attribute can only occur in conjunction with either the var or varReader attribute and defaults to page.

Both the jsp:doBody and jsp:invoke standard actions can have jsp:param standard actions as body content. The param actions can be used to initialize variables in a JSP fragment, allowing dynamic invocations.

6.2.3   Processing Variables in a Tag File

Sometimes a tag handler needs to expose a variable to the calling JSP page so information can be shared with other actions. One area in which this capability is useful is when tags need to cooperate, which is common in JSP applications that use the JSTL. Another area in which it is useful is when JSP fragments need access to data from the tag handler. This example can be applied to the right-banner JSP page to simplify the creation of the list of resources.

Example 6.7 right-banner.jsp

```
<%@ taglib prefix="pjbank" tagdir="/WEB-INF/tags" %>

<table class="border">

<pjbank:list>
<jsp:attribute name="dolist">
 <tr><td>
   <font class="start">${start}</font>
   <font class="rest">${rest}</font>
 </td></tr>
</jsp:attribute>
</pjbank:list>

</table>
```

This JSP page calls the list tag handler, passing the dolist JSP fragment that requires two variables, start and rest, to be initialized prior to being processed. The list tag handler is provided in the list.tag tag file.

Example 6.8 list.tag

```
<%@ taglib uri="http://java.sun.com/jstl/core_rt" prefix="c" %>
<%@ taglib uri="http://java.sun.com/jstl/xml_rt" prefix="x" %>
<%@ taglib uri="http://java.sun.com/jstl/fmt_rt" prefix="fmt" %>

<%@ attribute name="dolist" fragment="true" %>

<%@ variable name-given="start" scope="NESTED" %>
<%@ variable name-given="rest" scope="NESTED" %>
```

```
<c:import url="WEB-INF/xml/right-hand.xml" var="rhs" />
<x:parse xml="${rhs}" var="data" scope="request" />
<x:forEach var="item" select="$requestScope:data/items/*">

<c:set var="start">
 <x:out select="$item/start" />
</c:set>
<c:set var="rest">
 <x:out select="$item/rest" />
</c:set>

<jsp:invoke fragment="dolist" />

</x:forEach>
```

The list tag file first declares the dolist fragment attribute using the attribute directive. Following this, the start and rest variables are declared using the variable directive, which is detailed below. The list tag file uses the import tag in the JSTL core tag library to read the right-hand.xml file, and it uses the parse and forEach tags in the JSTL XML tag library to parse and iterate through this XML document that contains the information for the right-hand banner. The start and rest variables are initialized to the values of the start and rest child elements of each item element within the XML document. Once each of the variables is initialized, the JSP fragment dolist is invoked for each item. This approach allows the right-hand banner to be created dynamically, which might prove useful for displaying advertising or delivering real-time quotes.

The variable directive allows a developer to define variables that will be exposed by a tag handler in an identical format as the variable element in a TLD file. The variable directive has seven attributes, but it is only required to have one of the two different name attributes. Some combinations of these attributes result in translation errors, including the use of both name attributes, using the scope and fragment attributes together, and using the declare and fragment attributes together. In addition, variables must have unique names or a translation-time error is generated. The seven attributes of the variable directive are as follows.

- name-given is used to name an exported variable.
- name-from-attribute provides the name of an attribute whose run-time value names an exported variable.
- alias defines a locally scoped attribute to hold the value of this variable.
- variable-class provides the fully qualified class name, which defaults to java.lang.String, for the class of the variable.
- declare is a Boolean attribute used to indicate whether a variable is declared, which is the default.

- fragment is used to indicate whether a variable is scoped to a named JSP fragment or whether it appears in the body of the tag.
- scope attribute dictates the scope of the variable and can take on one of three values as follows:
  - AT_BEGIN indicates that the variable is available after the start tag until the end tag of any enclosing tag. If there is no enclosing tag, the variable is scoped to the end of the calling JSP page.
  - AT_END indicates that the variable is available after the end tag to any enclosing tag. If there is no enclosing tag, the variable is scoped to the end of the calling JSP page.
  - NESTED indicates that the variable is available only between the start and end tags. This is the default value.
- description provides an optional description of the variable.

With the introduction of the four tag files—header.tag, footer.tag, valid.tag, and list.tag—we can rewrite our welcome page, as shown in welcome.jsp and Figure 6.1. Although this JSP page does not appear significantly different than earlier versions, with the use of these four tag files, which are relatively straightforward to write, our Web application now uses no Java code. As a result, it is easier to maintain and develop.

Example 6.9 welcome.jsp

```jsp
<%@ page contentType="text/html" errorPage="exception.jsp" %>

<%@ taglib prefix="pjbank" tagdir="/WEB-INF/tags" %>

<pjbank:header title="Welcome to PJ Bank" />

<table width="100%">
 <tr>
  <td valign="top" width="25%"> <jsp:include page="left-banner.jsp" /> </td>
  <td valign="top">
   Welcome to PJ Bank, the persistent bank for those who like Java!
  </td>
  <td valign="top" width="25%"> <jsp:include page="right-banner.jsp" /> </td>
 </tr>
</table>

<pjbank:footer>
&copy; PJBank, 2002
</pjbank:footer>
```

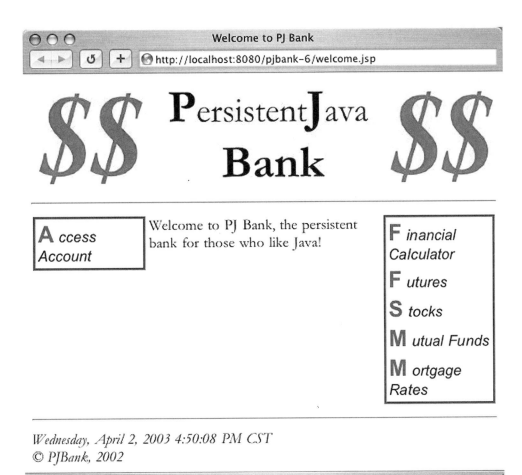

Figure 6.1: The rendered version of welcome.jsp after a successful log in.

6.3 Simple Tag Handlers

Although tag files do simplify the development of custom actions, sometimes a tag handler requires the power of the Java language or needs to use legacy code. If the tag does not need to support JSP scriptlet expressions, the tag can be implemented as a simple tag handler. The tag handler class can either implement the SimpleTag interface or extend the SimpleTagSupport base class.

6.3.1   SimpleTag Interface

The SimpleTag interface declares a single method, called doTag, that is called by the JSP container only once when the tag is encountered in a JSP page. Unlike the classic tag handler interfaces, which are described in the next section, the doTag method handles all tag processing internally. All tag logic, including any required iterations, is placed in this doTag method, which does not return any values. The tag handler has access to the tag's body content via the getJspBody method that returns a JspFragment object that contains the tag's body.

Simple tag handlers use a JspContext object to interact with the JSP container, unlike classic tag handlers, which use a PageContext object. As a result, simple tags are not dependent on the Servlet API. To export a variable, the setAttribute method is called on a JspContext object. If the tag handler determines that the JSP container should stop processing the calling JSP page, it throws a SkipPageException.

6.3.2   Implementing a Simple Tag Handler

To demonstrate writing a simple tag handler, the ListTag class extends the Simple TagSupport class to export fund information. To simplify the process, a JavaBean, AccountBean.java, is used to encapsulate the account information.

Example 6.10 AccountBean.java

```
package com.pjbank ;

import java.io.Serializable ;

public class AccountBean implements Serializable {

  private String name ;
  private int shares ;
  private double purchasePrice ;
  private double currentPrice ;

  public String getName() {
    return name;
    }

  public void setName(String value) {
    name = value ;
  }
...
}
```

Static information is used to populate a java.util.Vector with the account data, but the data could be pulled from a database, a file, or even a Web service. With the AccountBean, the ListTag class's doTag method sets this Vector as an attribute in the jspContext object, making it available to the calling JSP page. The compiled version of ListTag.java must follow the Java package naming sequence; in this case, that means the ListTag.class file must be in the com/pjbank/tags subdirectory of the Web application's WEB-INF/classes directory.

Example 6.11 ListTag.java

```java
package com.pjbank.tags;

import javax.servlet.jsp.JspException;
import javax.servlet.jsp.tagext.SimpleTagSupport;
import java.util.Vector;

import com.pjbank.AccountBean ;

public class ListAccountsTag extends SimpleTagSupport {

  private String[] name = {"Small Cap Fund","Asia Fund","Income Fund"} ;
  private int[] shares = {100, 250, 500} ;
  private double[] pprice = {21.25, 13.15, 24.50} ;
  private double[] cprice = {23.54, 18.74, 27.41} ;

  public void doTag() throws JspException {

    Vector accounts = new Vector() ;
    AccountBean account ;

    for(int i = 0 ; i < 3 ; i++){
      account = new AccountBean() ;
      account.setName(name[i]) ;
      account.setShares(shares[i]) ;
      account.setPurchasePrice(pprice[i]) ;
      account.setCurrentPrice(cprice[i]) ;

      accounts.add(account) ;

    }

    getJspContext().setAttribute("funds", accounts);
  }
}
```

Unlike tag files, tag handlers need TLD files to map a tag name to the implementation class. The TLD file, as discussed earlier, is an XML document written using XSD. The TLD file should be saved in the WEB-INF directory of the Web application that will use the tag handler.

For this example, our TLD file is relatively straightforward. First is the taglib element, which declares the relevant namespaces. Following this are several elements that provide basic information on our tag library, which in this case has the pjbank URI. Finally, the list tag is declared in the tag element, which contains three child elements that provide a name, the implementation class, and the content type of the tag's body.

Example 6.12 pjbank.tld

```
<taglib xmlns="http://java.sun.com/xml/ns/j2ee"
 xmlns:xsi="http://www.w3.org/2001/XMLSchema-instance"
 xsi:schemaLocation="http://java.sun.com/xml/ns/j2ee/web-jsptaglibrary_2_0.xsd"
 version="2.0">

  <tlib-version>1.2</tlib-version>
  <jsp-version>1.2</jsp-version>
  <short-name>pjbank</short-name>
  <uri>/pjbank</uri>

  <tag>
   <name>list</name>
   <tag-class>com.pjbank.tags.ListAccountsTag</tag-class>
   <body-content>empty</body-content>
  </tag>
</taglib>
```

To use a tag in a JSP page, it must be referenced using a taglib directive. For example, the following taglib directive will map the pjbank prefix to the pjbank-tag URI.

```
<%@ taglib uri="pjbank-tag" prefix="pjbank" %>
```

For the Web application to know which tag library the pjbank-tag URI is referencing, the Web application's deployment descriptor, web.xml, must provide an additional mapping. This multilevel mapping is detailed in Figure 6.2.

For the current example, this means a mapping between pjbank-tag URI and the pjbank.tld TLD file. This is demonstrated in web.xml, which is located in the WEB-INF directory.

Example 6.13 web.xml

```
<?xml version="1.0" encoding="ISO-8859-1"?>

<web-app xmlns="http://java.sun.com/xml/ns/j2ee"
```

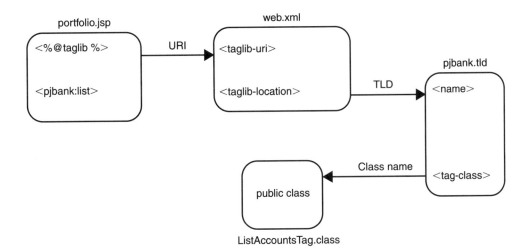

Figure 6.2: The mapping between tag usage, deployment descriptor, tag library descriptor, and the ListAccountsTag class.

```
xmlns:xsi="http://www.w3.org/2001/XMLSchema-instance"
xsi:schemaLocation="http://java.sun.com/xml/ns/j2ee web-app_2_4.xsd"
version="2.4">

<taglib>

 <taglib-uri>pjbank-tags</taglib-uri>
 <taglib-location>/WEB-INF/pjbank.tld</taglib-location>
</taglib>

</web-app>
```

After all this preparatory work, we can now use the list tag in a JSP page. The pjbank:list custom action exports a java.util.Vector to the calling JSP page that can be accessed to display account information. Once the funds vector has been created, we can iterate through it, displaying the relevant information as required, as shown in the following code example (this example is contained in full in portfolio.jsp in the pjbank-6 war file in the book's sample code).

```
<pjbank:list />
 <c:forEach var="fund" begin="0" items="${funds}">
  <tr>
   <td>${fund.name}</td>
```

```
        <c:set var="shares" value="${fund.shares}" />
        <td>${shares}</td>
...
    </tr>
   <c:set var="total" value="${total + cprice * shares}" />
</c:forEach>
```

This example could be extended to use an account number attribute to only return a single account. To use attributes, a tag handler class follows a JavaBean-like approach in which a class member is used to hold the attributes value, and a setter method named after the attribute's name is called to initialize the appropriate class member. For example if the attribute is named number, the tag handler class needs a setNumber method. The class member can be used in the tag's body. For example, a database query could be used to access a specific account.

6.4 Classic Tag Handlers

The original method for developing custom actions required experienced Java developers to implement tag handler classes. These classes could either extend support classes or implement interfaces, depending on the needs of the developer. With these three interfaces and support classes, a great deal of control is available to the tag developer. This control comes at the price of additional complexity. The rest of this section discusses these three interfaces in more detail and concludes with an example tag that processes its body content multiple times.

6.4.1 Tag Interface

The Tag interface can be used to create a tag handler that has a simple lifecycle, allowing special processing for the start and end of the tag. When a tag that implements the Tag interface is first encountered, it is initialized to have a reference to the current PageContext object and to any enclosing tag, which is called the *parent tag*. The PageContext object provides access to information about the JSP page that contains the tag.

After initialization, the doStartTag method is invoked. This method can return one of two values: SKIP_BODY or EVAL_BODY_INCLUDE. SKIP_BODY must be returned if the tag was declared to be empty in the TLD file, but it can also be used to conditionally evaluate a tag's body, similar to the if tag in the core JSTL tag library. If the JSP container should evaluate the body content, EVAL_BODY_INCLUDE should be returned instead.

Once the doStartTag has completed and, if required, after the tag's body has been processed, the doEndTag method is invoked. This method also can return one of two values: SKIP_PAGE or EVAL_PAGE. As their names suggest, these return values allow the tag to determine whether the rest of the page should be evaluated or not. If SKIP_PAGE is returned, only the evaluation of the current page is terminated, and the doEndTag methods of any enclosing tags are not processed. If the processing of the current page was the result of a forward or include action, processing will resume in the calling page.

6.4.2 IterationTag Interface

The IterationTag interface extends the Tag interface to provide support for multiple, sequential evaluations of a tag. The IterationTag interface provides the doAfterBody method, which is called after a tag's body content is evaluated by the JSP container. This method is only called if the doStartTag method returns EVAL_BODY_INCLUDE. The doAfterBody method can return two values—SKIP_BODY or EVAL_BODY_AGAIN—which indicate whether the tag's body should be reevaluated. If EVAL_BODY_AGAIN is returned, the body content is reevaluated; otherwise, the doEndTag method is called.

The TagSupport class is a utility class that provides a default implementation of the IterationTag interface that can be extended as needed by a tag developer. This class provides several convenience methods such as getParent, which provides access to the current tag's parent tag, and getValue and getValues, which provide access to the tag's properties. This class also provides the findAncestorWithClass method, which allows a tag developer to access a parent tag that implements a specific class.

6.4.3 BodyTag Interface

The BodyTag interface extends the IterationTag interface and, thus, the Tag interface as well. The BodyTag interface provides a tag developer with access to the tag's body content; however, any processing of the body content is left to the tag developer.

The BodyTag interface modifies the tag lifecycle of IterationTag by adding new methods and modifying inherited ones. The first change is that doStartTag can return a new value, EVAL_BODY_BUFFERED, which indicates to the JSP container that the tag's body will be made available to the tag handler class. This new value instructs the JSP container to create a BodyContent object that contains the evaluation of the tag's body content. As a result, any child tags or EL expressions are evaluated and the results made available to the tag handler class via the bodyContent property.

After the BodyContent object is initialized, a new method, doInitBody, which does not return any values, is called. This method will not be called for empty tags or if doStartTag returns SKIP_BODY. This method can be used to initialize state information that might depend on the tag's body content. The BodyTagSupport class is a utility class that provides a default implementation of the BodyTag interface.

6.4.4 Implementing a Classic Tag Handler

To demonstrate a classical tag handler, the following example, GetAccountTag.java, shows a tag handler that extends the TagSupport class to access a database and extract account information. This account information is made available to the calling JSP page via the AccountBean JavaBean, which was shown previously in this chapter. The database-specific code is identical to the database example from Chapter 5 and can easily be modified to use a JDBC DataSource or implement other specific capabilities. If this tag required access to its body content, the BodyTagSupport class would have been extended. However, in this case, the body content makes use of the fund attribute to access the current account before the tag makes the next iteration.

Example 6.14 GetAccountTag.java

```java
package com.pjbank.tags;

import java.sql.* ;
import javax.servlet.jsp.JspException;
import javax.servlet.jsp.tagext.TagSupport;

import com.pjbank.AccountBean ;

public class GetAccountTag extends TagSupport {

  private final static String url = "jdbc:mysql://localhost/pjbank";

  private final static String selectQuery = "SELECT * FROM portfolio" ;

  private final static String user = "jack" ;
  private final static String passwd = "jill" ;

  private Connection con ;
  private Statement stmt ;
  private ResultSet rs ;

  private AccountBean account ;

  public int doStartTag() throws JspException {

    try {
      Class.forName("com.mysql.jdbc.Driver") ;
      con = DriverManager.getConnection(url, user, passwd) ;
      stmt = con.createStatement() ;
      rs = stmt.executeQuery(selectQuery) ;

      return(doGetRow(EVAL_BODY_INCLUDE)) ;
    } catch (Exception e) {
      throw new JspException(e.getMessage()) ;
    }
  }

  public int doAfterBody() throws JspException {
    return (doGetRow(EVAL_BODY_AGAIN)) ;
```

```
  }

  public int doEndTag() throws JspException {
    try{
      rs.close() ;
      stmt.close() ;
      con.close() ;
    } catch (SQLException e) {
      throw new JspException(e.getMessage()) ;
    }
    return(EVAL_PAGE) ;
  }

  public int doGetRow(int evalType) throws JspException {
    try{
      if(rs.next()){
        account = new AccountBean() ;
        account.setName(rs.getString(1)) ;
        account.setShares(rs.getInt(2)) ;
        account.setPurchasePrice(rs.getDouble(3)) ;
        account.setCurrentPrice(rs.getDouble(4)) ;

        pageContext.setAttribute("fund", account);
        return(evalType) ;
      }else
        return(SKIP_BODY) ;
    } catch (Exception e) {
      throw new JspException(e.getMessage()) ;
    }
  }
}
```

In this tag handler, the doStartTag method first establishes the database connection and executes the query. The AccountBean initialization code has been factored out into the doGetRow method, which processes the current valid row from the database. If the current row is not valid, SKIP_BODY is returned; otherwise, the evaluation type passed in to the doGetRow method, either EVAL_BODY_INCLUDE or EVAL_BODY_AGAIN, is returned after the AccountBean has been added as an attribute to the PageContext object. The doAfterBody simply calls the doGetRow method, while the doEndTag method cleans up the database-specific resources. The lifecycle of GetAccountTag is shown in Figure 6.3.

To use this tag, it must be added to the pjbank.tld TLD file. The specific addition is shown on the next page and consists of the tag name (get) and the tag handler's implementation class (com.pjbank.tags.GetAccountTag). Because this TLD file is already referenced

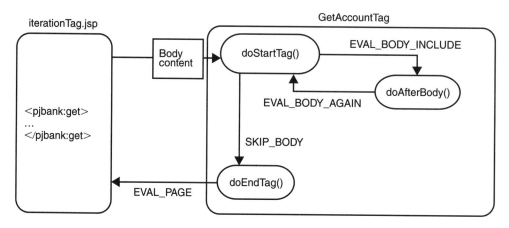

Figure 6.3: The GetAccountTag lifecycle.

in our Web application's deployment descriptor, the web.xml file does not need to be modified.

```
<tag>
 <name>get</name>
 <tag-class>com.pjbank.tags.GetAccountTag</tag-class>
 <body-content>JSP</body-content>
</tag>
```

Now that the GetAccountTag is available, we can use it in a JSP page, as shown below in the partial listing for iterationTag.jsp. First, the database connection is made when the <pjbank:get> start tag is encountered by the doStartTag method. If the database contains any account information, the next step is to process the body content, which in this case is to display the fund information. Otherwise, the body content is not processed.

After the body content is processed, the doAfterBody method is called, which in this case means the next account is accessed. The loop of processing body content and calling doAfterBody continues until all accounts have been displayed. At this point the doAfterBody method returns SKIP_BODY and the doEndTag method is called, which releases the database connection. The resulting Web page is shown in Figure 6.4.

Example 6.15 iterationTag.jsp

```
...
<pjbank:get>
 <tr>
  <td>${fund.name}</td>
  <c:set var="shares" value="${fund.shares}" />
  <td>${shares}</td>
```

Figure 6.4: The GetAccountTag displaying account information.

```
<c:set var="pprice" value="${fund['purchasePrice']}" />
<td><fmt:formatNumber value="${pprice}" type="currency"/></td>
<c:set var="cprice" value="${fund['currentPrice']}" />
<td><fmt:formatNumber value="${cprice}" type="currency"/></td>
<td><fmt:formatNumber value="${cprice * shares}" type="currency"/></td>
</tr>
<c:set var="total" value="${total + cprice * shares}" />
</pjbank:get>
...
```

Exercises

1. Describe the difference between a tag file and a tag handler, including a discussion of when to use each.

2. Write a tag file that displays the contents of a ShoppingCartBean.

3. Write a tag file that summarizes the contents of a ShoppingCartBean and displays the total cost for the shopping cart's contents.

4. Write a simple tag handler that returns a shipping cost based on a zip code, which can be passed to the tag handler via either the tag's body or an attribute. The actual formula used is arbitrary; the tag logic is what is important for this problem.

5. Describe the difference between the BodyTag and IterationTag interfaces.

6. Write a classic tag handler that extends the BodyTagSupport class to convert the tag's body to uppercase characters.

chapter **7**

Building a Web Application

Throughout this book, JavaServer Pages technology has been used to build interactive Web applications. However, JSP is only one—although a very important one—part of the available suite of technologies that can be used to build production-quality Web applications. Other technologies, such as Java Servlets, JavaScript, Cascading Style Sheets (CSS), and security, are often important components in building a successful Web application. This chapter introduces these topics and demonstrates how they can be successfully combined with JSP technology.

7.1   Java Servlet Technology

Servlet technology was the first Java solution for generating dynamic Web content. Prior to the introduction of Java Servlets, most dynamic Web content was produced by common gateway interface (CGI) programs, which were written in C or Perl. Although these were easy for advanced developers to write, the average Web developer did not possess the skills required to develop CGI applications. In addition, early CGI applications were often buggy and insecure. Finally, they were inherently non-portable, as they often were compiled into native machine code for increased performance.

With the introduction of Java Servlets, many of these difficulties were reduced or eliminated altogether. Being written in Java, Servlets were portable across any Web server that provided support for Java Server applications. In addition, Servlets used the Java security model and had access to Java APIs that simplified the use of databases.

As you will see, however, Servlets are not the best solution for generating presentation material, such as HTML Web pages. The creation of such pages was one of the primary drivers for the creation of JSP. The rest of this section introduces Java Servlets and demonstrates how they can be used within JSP-based Web applications.

7.1.1 Servlet Overview

Java Servlets were introduced in Chapter 1, in which the Servlet lifecycle was first discussed. This early introduction demonstrates the importance of Servlets to JSP applications. After all, a JSP page is translated into a Servlet. Thus, understanding Servlets is required for an in-depth understanding of JSP.

The actual Servlet API reflects its lifecycle in the GenericServlet class with init, service, and destroy methods, which correspond to the init, service, and destroy lifecycle events. This class is useful for implementing a service that responds to a generic service request. Most Web applications, however, explicitly use Hypertext Transport Protocol (HTTP). The Servlet API includes the HttpServlet class for these applications. This class provides methods such as doGet and doPost for handling HTTP requests like GET or POST, respectively. The Servlet API also provides a mechanism for handling lifecycle events, such as initialization, destruction, and session management, via listener interfaces, which allows a developer to maintain fine-grained control of a Web application. Finally, Servlets provide JSP applications with the ability to generate responses that contain different types of content.

In the drive to remove Java code from JSP documents, Servlets play an important role. Formally, using Servlets in a JSP Web application enables a new model for Web-application development, known as Model 2, or Model View Controller (MVC). This model has a Servlet functioning as the controller, in which requests are analyzed, potentially processed, and directed to a suitable JSP page, where the presentation, or view, is generated.

To register a Servlet with a Web application, it must be declared in the application's deployment descriptor, and the Servlet name must be mapped to a particular Universal Resource Locator (URL). The first step is accomplished using the servlet element, which maps a name to an implementation class. The second step is performed by the servlet-mapping element, which maps the Servlet name to a URL pattern. For example, the following demonstrates associating the name control to a Servlet and mapping it to the /control URL.

```
<servlet>
 <servlet-name>control</servlet-name>
 <servlet-class>com.pjbank.ControlServlet</servlet-class>
</servlet>

<servlet-mapping>
 <servlet-name>control</servlet-name>
 <url-pattern>/control</url-pattern>
</servlet-mapping>
```

Another useful capability the Servlet API provides to the JSP developer is a Filter, which can preprocess a request or postprocess a response. Filters can be used to modify the headers or data contained in the request or the response, block requests or responses, and interact with external resources. As a result, Filters can be used for authentication, logging, content conversion, compression, encryption, or transformation. Filters can also be chained together, which allows modular Filters to be composited to build more complex Filters.

As with Servlets, Filters must be declared in the Web application's deployment descriptor. Both a `filter` and `filter-mapping` elements are used, analogous to the `servlet` and `servlet-mapping` elements, to map a Filter name to an implementation class and associate it with a URL pattern. For example, the following shows how to register the Filter named `blockloan` to its implementation class and map it to the /control URL.

```
<filter>
 <filter-name>blockloan</filter-name>
 <filter-class>com.pjbank.BlockLoanFilter</filter-class>
</filter>

<filter-mapping>
 <filter-name>blockloan</filter-name>
 <url-pattern>/control</url-pattern>
</filter-mapping>
```

7.1.2 The Servlet Controller

The first area in which Servlet technology is useful when building a JSP Web application is in providing controller functionality. The controller works as its name suggests, controlling traffic and directing requests to the appropriate response handler. This is demonstrated in Figure 7.1, in which the Servlet controller acts like an air traffic controller. The client's request is routed to the Servlet, where it is directed to an appropriate JSP page, depending on the type of request, where the response is generated and returned to the client.

This approach is demonstrated in ControlServlet.java, in which the process Request method directs the request to a JSP page determined at run-time, based on the action attribute in the client's HTTP request. This example also demonstrates several other important points. First, this Servlet extends the HttpServlet class, which allows it to process HTTP requests. Second, the doGet and doPost methods forward request processing to a single method, called processRequest, which handles all requests. This provides a single path of execution, which in our case is sufficient because POST and GET requests should be handled identically. Finally, this example shows how Servlets and JSP pages can collaborate by both sharing data via parameters and attributes and forwarding requests appropriately.

The actual processRequest method grabs the action parameter from the request headers, and if it is not null, the method creates a RequestDispatcher object that can be used to forward a request from a Servlet to a JSP page. In this case, the actual JSP page is constructed dynamically from the name of the action and the *.jsp* file extension. Notice that

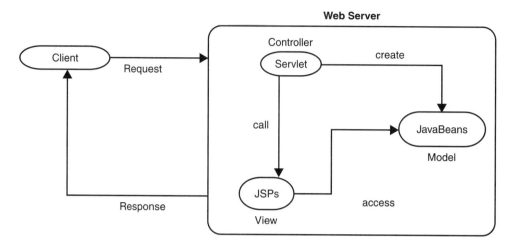

Figure 7.1: The MVC approach to using Servlets and JSPs together.

although not required, appending Servlet to the name of the implementation class is a useful visual aid to the class's intended function.

This simple example does not perform any request processing; however, doing so is simple. Request headers can be accessed, JavaBeans created, and new attributes added to the request, allowing the response to be customized appropriately. Although this example shows only a single Servlet, in reality, multiple Servlets are often used to do the back-end processing, possibly in conjunction with Enterprise JavaBeans (EJBs), directing different JSP pages to generate the appropriate responses.

Example 7.1 ControlServlet.java

```
package com.pjbank;

import javax.servlet.*;
import javax.servlet.http.*;

public class ControlServlet extends HttpServlet {

  protected void processRequest(HttpServletRequest request,
    HttpServletResponse response)
    throws ServletException, java.io.IOException {
    String action =request.getParameter("action") ;

    if(action == null)
       throw new ServletException("No Action Specified") ;

    RequestDispatcher dispatcher = request.getRequestDispatcher(action+".jsp") ;
```

```
    dispatcher.forward(request, response) ;

  }

  protected void doGet(HttpServletRequest request, HttpServletResponse response)
  throws ServletException, java.io.IOException {
    processRequest(request, response);
  }

  protected void doPost(HttpServletRequest request, HttpServletResponse response)
  throws ServletException, java.io.IOException {
    processRequest(request, response);
  }
}
```

To demonstrate this Servlet in action, welcome.jsp generates a simple Web page that provides three URLs, which are identical except for a different value of the action request
parameter: stocks, funds, or loans. The ControlServlet is mapped in web.xml, using the
XML deployment descriptor shown in the previous section. Thus, the /control URL used
in welcome.jsp directs the request to the controller Servlet.

Example 7.2 welcome.jsp

```
<%@ page contentType="text/html" errorPage="exception.jsp" isELIgnored="false"%>
<%@ taglib uri="http://java.sun.com/jstl/core_rt" prefix="c" %>

<%@ taglib prefix="pjbank" tagdir="/WEB-INF/tags" %>

<pjbank:header title="Welcome to PJ Bank" />

<table width="100%">
 <tr>
  <c:url value="control" var="url">
   <c:param name="action" value="stocks"/>
  </c:url>
  <td> <a href="${url}">Stock Listing</a> </td>
 </tr>
 <tr>
  <c:url value="control" var="url">
   <c:param name="action" value="funds"/>
  </c:url>
  <td> <a href="${url}">Mutual Fund Listing</a> </td>
 </tr>
 <tr>
```

```
<c:url value="control" var="url">
 <c:param name="action" value="loans"/>
</c:url>
<td> <a href="${url}">Loan Information</a> </td>
</tr>
</table>

<pjbank:footer>
&copy; PJBank, 2002
</pjbank:footer>
```

For each different action, we need a JSP page to generate the actual response. Because they are all similar, only one of the three response JSP pages is listed here (the others are included in the book's sample code). As can be seen in loans.jsp, a fictitious table showing different loan possibilities is displayed. In production systems, this table would be generated dynamically, probably from database or Web service calls. The resulting loan information is displayed in Figure 7.2. Notice how the URL shown in the Web browser is not loans.jsp. The ability of an MVC application to hide the use of an actual Web-application resource is an interesting side effect, as clients are unaware of the details of the Web application—an important security benefit.

Example 7.3 loans.jsp

```
<%@ page contentType="text/html" errorPage="exception.jsp" isELIgnored="false"%>

<%@ taglib prefix="pjbank" tagdir="/WEB-INF/tags" %>

<pjbank:header title="Loan Information" />

<h2> Loan Information </h2>
<hr/>
<table border="2">
 <tr> <th>Loan Term</th> <th>Current Rate</th> </tr>
 <tr> <td>30 Year Fixed</td> <td>5.875</td></tr>
 <tr> <td>20 Year Fixed</td> <td>5.625</td></tr>
 <tr> <td>15 Year Fixed</td> <td>5.40</td></tr>
 <tr> <td>7 Year ARM/30 Year Term</td> <td>5.25</td></tr>
 <tr> <td>5 Year ARM/30 Year Term</td> <td>5.125</td></tr>
</table>
<pjbank:footer>
&copy; PJBank, 2002
</pjbank:footer>
```

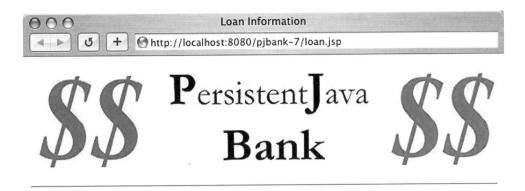

Figure 7.2: The loan information JSP page, showing the result of the controller Servlet.

7.1.3 The Servlet Filter

The second useful Servlet API capability for a JSP developer is the ability to filter requests and responses. This is demonstrated by the BlockLoanFilter class, which can be used in conjunction with the controller Servlet shown in the previous section to block all loan information requests. Again, appending "Filter" to the end of the implementation class's name is a useful aid in understanding the class's purpose.

BlockLoanFilter implements the javax.servlet.Filter interface. This implies that the init and destroy methods must be implemented, as well as the doFilter method. For this simple example, the init and destroy methods are empty, but they can be used to initialize and finalize external resources as needed. In addition, the doFilter method is very similar to the processRequest method from the ControlServlet.

Because the Filter interface is designed to interact with arbitrary protocol requests, the first step is to cast the request object to an HTTP request. This is necessary to access the HTTP action parameter. If the action parameter is not null and is equal to loans, the request is redirected to the noloans.jsp page. Otherwise this filter does nothing to the request, which proceeds normally through the Servlet controller. One other important point about doFilter is the FilterChain input parameter. This allows a Web application to chain filters together.

Example 7.4 BlockLoanFilter.java

```
package com.pjbank;

import javax.servlet.*;
import javax.servlet.http.*;

public class BlockLoanFilter implements Filter {

  public void init(FilterConfig config) throws ServletException {
  }

  public void destroy() {
  }

  public void doFilter(ServletRequest request, ServletResponse response,
      FilterChain chain)
      throws java.io.IOException, ServletException {
    HttpServletRequest req = (HttpServletRequest)request ;

    String action =req.getParameter("action") ;

    if(action == null)
      throw new ServletException("No Action Specified") ;
    else if(action.equals("loans")) {

      RequestDispatcher dispatcher = request.getRequestDispatcher("noloans.jsp") ;
      dispatcher.forward(request, response) ;
    }
  }
}
```

For this Filter to be used in a Web application, it must be defined in the application's deployment descriptor and mapped to a URL. This was shown earlier in the chapter (and can be

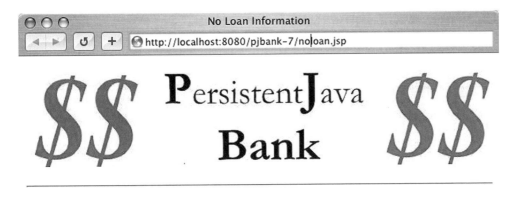

Figure 7.3: The noloans.jsp page, showing the effect of the BlockLoanFilter.

demonstrated by removing the appropriate comments from the deployment descriptor in the sample code). Once the appropriate XML elements have been added to the web.xml deployment descriptor, the BlockLoanFilter is ready for action. To complete the example, the noloans.jsp page displays a warning message that loan information is currently unavailable, as shown in Figure 7.3.

Example 7.5 noloans.jsp

```
<%@ page contentType="text/html" errorPage="exception.jsp" isELIgnored="false"%>

<%@ taglib prefix="pjbank" tagdir="/WEB-INF/tags" %>

<pjbank:header title="No Loan Information" />

<h2> We're sorry, but the loan information is currently unavailable. </h2>
<pjbank:footer>
&copy; PJBank, 2003
</pjbank:footer>
```

7.2 Ancillary Web-Application Technologies

Although this book is formally concerned with JSP, building Web applications often requires myriad technologies, including those from the Servlet API that were introduced previously. This section details several other technologies that are often vital to building useable Web applications. The end of this section discusses the benefit of Web-application frameworks in simplifying the incorporation of these technologies for application developers.

7.2.1 Cascading Style Sheets

HTML was originally devised as a language that could be used to markup a document, primarily to describe its content. For example, tags were used to mark paragraphs, titles, and lists. As Web browsers became more powerful, content providers wanted better control over how a document was presented to a client. This desire led to the addition of more—often browser customized—tags, such as font, which had nothing to do with the content of the document and instead dictated how a document should be presented.

This tight coupling between a document and the way it should be presented complicated the development and resulting maintenance of Web sites. First, a Web site designer had to know how to control the appearance of a Web page across multiple Web browsers. Even more difficult was the targeting of potentially new clients, such as personal data assistants or cellular telephones. Second, if the presentation needed to be changed, all the Web pages had to be modified because the presentation was encoded within the Web page itself. Not only does this make it harder to change the way a Web site appears to clients, but it also makes it more likely that bugs or presentation errors will be introduced.

The obvious solution is to separate the markup responsible for describing what is in a document from the markup that describes how a document should be presented to a client. The World Wide Web Consortium (W3C) accomplished this goal with the introduction of Cascading Style Sheets (CSS).[1] The CSS specifications provide a large measure of control over how a Web page should be presented. Many modern Web browsers provide support for the majority of the CSS recommendations, and support continues to grow. The rest of this section discusses the basics of CSS and presents a simple style sheet that has been used in this book for the PJ Bank Web application. This style sheet is designed only to demonstrate how a style sheet can be used within a Web application and is not intended as a demonstration of good visual design. In a production system, a professional graphic artist or Web designer should be consulted to ensure a high-impact Web application.

CSS uses a simple syntax for associating style rules with an element. Basically, the CSS syntax uses a *selector*, which determines which element will be styled, followed by a list of style properties and their desired values.

---

[1] The official W3C site for CSS technology is *http://www.w3.org/Style/CSS.*

```
selector {
propertyOne: valueOne;
propertyTwo: valueTwo;
propertyThree: valueThree;
...
}
```

For example, the following selector shows a paragraph element for displaying a paragraph in uppercase characters, all in red, with a line over the text.

```
p {
color: #FF0000;
text-transform: uppercase;
text-decoration: overline
}
```

This style can be associated with a single paragraph element using the style attribute.

```
<p style="color: #FF0000; text-transform: uppercase; text-decoration: overline">
Here is a special paragraph.
</p>
```

Alternatively, this style can be specified for all paragraph elements within a Web page by placing this style definition inside a style element, which belongs inside the head element.

```
<head>
 <style type="text/css">
  p {
  color: #FF0000;
  text-transform: uppercase;
  text-decoration: overline
  }
 </style>
</head>
<p> Here is a special paragraph </p>
```

Finally, this style, along with many other style specifications, can be placed in an external style sheet and linked to multiple Web pages. This is the generally recommended approach, as it easily allows multiple Web pages to share the same styling, which simplifies the development and maintenance of the resulting Web application.

```
<head>
 <link rel="stylesheet" type="text/css" href="style/pstyle.css" />
</head>
<p> Here is a special paragraph </p>
```

These previous examples demonstrate the different techniques with which a style can be associated with an element. When determining the appropriate style for a specific element, a style is selected (or, for an entire document, the style sheet is constructed) by cascading down the following four mechanisms (in this order) for attaching a style to an

HTML element:

1. style attached directly to the element via `style` attribute
2. style attached inside the head element of a Web page
3. style listed in an external style sheet linked to the Web page
4. style reverts to the browser's default style

The previous CSS examples demonstrate how a style can be associated with a single element type. The CSS specification also allows a style to be associated with multiple elements, via the `class` attribute, or a specific element, via the `id` attribute. For example, the `class` attribute can be used to specify that some paragraph elements should be written using the Garamond font, while others should use the Arial font. First, the selectors must be declared.

```
p.garamond {font-family: garamond}
p.arial {font-family: arial}
```

Once these font styles have been included into the document, perhaps via an external style sheet, they can be used by including the `class` attribute with the appropriate element.

```
<p class="garamond"> Here is Garamond </p>
<p class = "arial"> Here is Arial </p>
```

A class selector can also be declared across multiple elements by dropping the element name from the declaration. This allows for an arbitrary Garamond font selector.

```
.garamond {font-family: garamond}
```

The `id` attribute can be used to target a specific element to style. The `id` attribute selector is declared in a similar manner to the `class` attribute selector.

```
p#garamond {font-family: garamond}
```

This style can be applied to an element with the `id` attribute.

```
<p id="garamond"> Here is Garamond </p>
```

Although not complete, this simple introduction provides enough detail to build a simple style sheet for the PJ Bank Web application, which is shown in `pjbank.css`. This example only requires three selectors: one for specifying the border around the components of the master Web page and two for controlling the font types and sizes of the left and right banner text. In this example, multiple values are provided for the `font-family` property, which can be important because some browsers may not have the first font listed.

Example 7.6 style/pjbank.css

```
.border {
border-style: groove;
}
```

```
.start {
font-family: arial, times ;
font-size: 150%;
font-weight: bolder;
color: #006600
}

.rest {
font-family: arial, times ;
font-size: 100%;
font-style: oblique;
}
```

7.2.2 JavaScript and Form Validation

Another important concept for building a successful Web application is the task of validating user input. Although final verification must always be done at the server (for example, to validate a successful user login), verifying user input at the client can be an important mechanism for reducing the processing load on your application server.

One of the most dominant mechanisms for validating user input at the client is to use JavaScript[2] along with the inherent event notification features built into HTML. JavaScript is very similar to Java, which makes it easy for JSP developers to use. The biggest departure of JavaScript from Java is probably that its variables are dynamically typed. In practice, this means that all variables are declared to be of type var, but they can be assigned a value from any legal datatype.

As in Java, JavaScript objects can be created with properties and methods. Certain useful objects are built into the language, and Web browsers that support JavaScript provide extra built-in objects. These JavaScript objects in the browser make the contents of the current Web page accessible to a JavaScript program, which allows the contents of a Web page to change dynamically without any input from the server. JavaScript also provides simple functions that can be called to create a pop-up window to alert the user, ask for confirmation, or prompt for certain input.

For the PJ Bank Web application, we are primarily interested in validating user input. This requires the introduction of three relevant concepts: defining a function in JavaScript, attaching a JavaScript function to an HTML event, and including JavaScript in a Web page.

Defining a function is a simple task in JavaScript and is shown in the following example. Because JavaScript provides access to the contents of a Web page, including all form

---

[2]This is formally known as ECMAScript after the European Computer Manufacturers Association, a standards group that generated a standard definition. See *http://www.ecma-international.org/publications/files/ecma-st/Ecma-262.pdf* for more information.

data, validation is easy. This function checks that a user entered a number between one and 10 in the guess input control of the game form. If the value is out of the allowed range, an alert window is raised; otherwise, the function does nothing.

```
function validateGuess() {

  var guess = document.game.guess.value ;
  if((guess < 1)||(guess > 10)) {
   alert("Your guess must be a number between one and ten.") ;
   return false ;
  }
  return true ;
}
```

To be useful, this function needs to be called before the data is sent to the server, which is easily done by calling this function when the "submit" button is clicked. This is just one of many different intrinsic events that are defined as part of the HTML standard.[3] The form element accepts an onsubmit attribute, which can be used to call this function when the form is submitted.

```
<form name="game" onsubmit="return validateGuess()" >
<input type="text" name="guess">
<input type="submit" value="Submit">
</form>
```

In a Web page that has this form, the validateGuess function is called whenever the user clicks the "submit" button. If the guessed value is within the allowed range, the form is submitted (although no action was actually specified in this example). If the guess is outside the allowed range, an alert window is displayed with an informative message, and the form is not submitted.

Of course, for the function to be called, it must be available to the Web page. This can be done by either including the script within the Web page or by linking to an external script file. To include JavaScript within a Web page, it must be placed inside a script element, which should be placed inside the head element to guarantee that the scripts are available as soon as the Web page is loaded by the browser.

```
<head>
 <script type="text/javascript">
  function validateGuess() {
...

  }
 </script>
</head>
```

---

[3] The complete list of intrinsic events can be found at *http://www.w3.org/TR/html4/interact/scripts. html#h-18.2.3.*

Although useful when initially building and testing Web pages, the better (and recommended) solution when building Web applications is to place all JavaScript code in a separate file. This promotes code reuse and simplifies making changes whenever necessary. To link an external script file into a Web page, the script element is used with the src attribute indicating the location of the script file.

```
<head>
 <script src="scripts/myscript.js" />
</head>
```

For the PJ Bank application, the username and password fields should contain actual data before the request is sent to the server. This requires only small changes from the guess example, as shown in login.js. Although more logic could be encoded in this function, or even split across multiple functions (one for the username and one for the password, for example), the simplicity of adding control logic at the client is still demonstrated.

Example 7.7 login.js

```
function validate() {
 var uname = document.loginForm.username.value ;
 var pword = document.loginForm.password.value ;

 if(uname.length == 0) {
  alert("Please enter a Username") ;
  return false ;
 }

 if(pword.length == 0) {
  alert("Please enter a Password") ;
  return false ;
 }

 return true ;
}
```

The results of invoking this method were shown previously in Chapter 3.

7.2.3 Web-Application Frameworks

The step from developing a simple JSP-based Web application to building production-level Web applications is not small. JSP pages must be combined with JavaBeans, tag libraries, style sheets, JavaScript functions, and even Servlets. Keeping track of everything can be difficult, and ensuring that everything works together appropriately can be even harder. To simplify the task of a developer in building Web applications, several frameworks have been created. One of the most popular is the Struts framework from the Apache Software Foundation.

A complete description of the Struts framework is beyond the scope of this book,[4] but a brief overview is certainly in order. The Struts framework encourages developers to build MVC, or Model 2, Web applications because it supplies its own controller Servlet. The model is often encapsulated by JavaBeans, and presentation-focused JSP pages handle the view. To handle new actions, classes are built that follow a specific pattern. These classes have a name that ends in *.do*, which is mapped in the deployment descriptor to the controller Servlet. Struts also simplifies the development of HTML forms, along with possible client-side verification.

One of the concerns with Struts, as well as with other Java-based Web-application frameworks, is the lack of standardization within the community and among Web-application servers. This has been addressed by the Java Community Process, which is developing JavaServer Faces (JSF) technology.[5] JSF has many similarities to Struts, as it provides a standard API for handling all aspects of the user interface components needed by a Web application. These components are provided as a custom tag library and are easily used within a Web application.

7.3 Security

The Internet provides many benefits, but one of its primary disadvantages is the very open nature that makes it so useful. Being open to clients means being open to attacks as well. To keep information and resources safe, Web applications must employ various security strategies. The Servlet specification details four requirements that a server must provide to a Web application:

1. *Authentication:* Clients and servers must be able to verify that the other parties they encounter are who they say they are.

2. *Access Control:* Access to resources must be controlled. Only those who should be able to access a resource must be able to do so.

3. *Integrity:* Data and information must not be modified outside the Web application.

4. *Confidentiality:* Access to information is restricted to only those who have sufficient access rights.

When building a Web application using JSP technology, there are essentially two approaches to providing security for these four requirements: *programmatic security* and

---

[4]The Struts framework, including extensive online documentation, is available at *http://jakarta. apache.org/struts*.
[5]The official home for JSF technology is *http://java.sun.com/j2ee/javaserverfaces*.

declarative security. The difference between these two approaches, which can be combined, is that programmatic security places the burden on the application developer, while declarative security uses the deployment descriptor to declare specific security procedures.

To understand how resources and information can be controlled, Web applications often use the concepts of *roles*, *users*, and *groups*. A user is a specific person, a role is a category of users that share common features, and a group is comprised of users that may belong to different roles. These concepts may be easier to understand if you think about the security of a building. Users are people that work in the building. A role corresponds to functions a person may perform within the building, such as management or staff, which have different security levels. Groups of people may also have access to certain resources, like a conference room, depending on the needs of the organization.

7.3.1 Programmatic Security

Programmatic security is conceptually the easiest to understand, as it is what we have been using with the PJ Bank Web application throughout this book. The burden for performing security is placed on the Web-application developer. Although this extra burden does complicate the development process, the benefit is that the application is less dependent on a particular application server than it would be with the alternative approach.

Two simple methods for developing custom security solutions are building a security custom tag library or using a Filter. In either case, access rights must be checked prior to accessing the resource. If the user is authenticated, the resource can be provided; otherwise, an error condition is signaled and appropriate action must be taken. For example, we could use a pjbank:security tag that called the isValid method on the LoginBean.

```
<pjbank:security />
```

If the user is validated, processing can continue normally. Otherwise, an error page should be returned that allows the user to log in and be redirected to the appropriate page. Placing this tag at the start of a JSP page that requires authentication allows this capability to be easily added to an application. However, the onus is entirely on the application developer. Forgetting to use this tag would not result in an error, only a security hole. Using a Filter reduces this risk, as the Filter can be mapped to a URL pattern, which might be the entire application. On the other hand, Filters can be more difficult to write.

7.3.2 Declarative Security

Declarative security, on the other hand, minimizes the burden on an application developer, as it requires the JSP container to manage the application's security. Because the JSP and Servlet specifications do not completely define the mechanisms for a container to provide security, this approach is less portable. The biggest area in which this limitation is evident is in the definition of users and roles. For example, the Apache Tomcat server uses a separate XML document to hold user and role definitions. The Tomcat server also provides *realms*, which can be backed by a database to maintain this information. Moving to a different application server requires transforming these information repositories into a format suitable to the new server.

Security is applied to resources using the security-constraint element within the application's deployment descriptor. Within this element, the auth-constraint element is used to restrict access to specific resources to a given role. For example, the following XML code restricts access to the /pjbank URL to only the manager role.

```
<security-constraint>
 <web-resource-collection>
  <web-resource-name>PJ Bank Web Application</web-resource-name>
  <url-pattern>/pjbank</url-pattern>
 </web-resource-collection>

 <auth-constraint>
  <role-name>manager</role-name>
 </auth-constraint>
</ security-constraint>
```

The Servlet specification[6] defines three authentication methods—*Basic*, *Digest*, and *Form* only one of which can be used within a given Web application. Both Basic and Digest authentication mechanisms are defined as part of the HTTP specification; they require a Web browser to open an external dialog that allows the user to enter a username and password. The type of authentication is specified using the login-config element within the deployment descriptor. For example, the following XML can be used to specify that an application will use HTTP Digest authentication.

```
<login-config>
 <auth-method>DIGEST</auth-method>
 <realm-name>PJ Bank Web Application</realm-name>
</login-config>
```

HTTP Basic authentication transmits the username and password from the client to the server as part of the HTTP request using Base64 encoding. This approach is very insecure, as the HTTP request can be easily intercepted and the encoded data easily decoded, providing access to valid username/password combinations.

HTTP Digest authentication, on the other hand, encrypts the password before transmitting it to the server as part of the HTTP request. This makes the task of stealing a password more difficult, but not impossible. Another problem with Digest authentication is that fewer Web browsers provide support for it, and assisting the client when improper credentials are entered is very difficult.

---

[6]Security is discussed in Chapter 12 of the Servlet specification, which is available online from *http://java.sun.com/products/servlet.*

These problems are greatly reduced with Form-based authentication. Form-based authentication allows an application developer to use an HTML form, which can be embedded within a JSP page to authenticate a user. This means the information presented to the user can be customized, and it allows the application to easily assist a user in recovering lost passwords or usernames. Form-based authentication requires extra information, however, and the developer must follow a prescribed pattern when creating the login form.

First, the form element must specify an action attribute with the value of j_security_check. The input elements used to acquire the username and password must also have name attributes that are specified as j_username and j_password, respectively.

```
<form method="post" action ="j_security_check" >
 <fieldset>
 <legend>Login Information</legend>
 <table>
 <tr>
  <td><label for="uname">User Name:</label></td>
  <td><input type="text" name ="j_username" id="uname"></td>
 </tr>
 <tr>
  <td><label for="pword">Password:</label></td>
  <td><input type="password" name ="j_password" id="pword"></td>
 </tr>
 </table>
 <p/><input type="submit" value="Login">
     <input type="reset">
 </fieldset>
</form>
```

Second, the application's deployment descriptor must have an extra section that defines a login JSP page and an error JSP page that will be called as needed.

```
<login-config>
 <auth-method>FORM</auth-method>
 <form-login-config>
  <form-login-page>/login.jsp</form-login-page>
  <form-error-page>/error.jsp</form-error-page>
 </form-login-config>
 <realm-name>PJ Bank Web Application</realm-name>
</login-config>
```

Once the login and error pages are written, the Form-based authentication method is complete, and the rest of the application can be developed.

7.3.3 Secure Sockets Layer

While all three of the previous techniques (Basic, Digest, and Form based authentication) simplified the authentication procedure, application data is still open to interception as its transmitted across the Internet. To prevent unauthorized viewing of confidential data, the request and the response must be encrypted. To accomplish this, a Web application must use HTTP over Secure Sockets, or HTTPS.

To use HTTPS, the server (and possibly the client) needs to have a security certificate. A security certificate is used by a server to verify its identity to a client. As long as the client trusts the certificate, which is traditionally obtained from a third-party corporation, such as Verisign or Thawte, a secure channel can be established. This third party will verify the identity of an individual or corporation, allowing the client to more easily work with many different servers. By default, many browsers automatically trust certificates signed by a small cadre of security companies.

As the verification process can be lengthy, it is not free. For demonstration purposes, however, an easier route to generating an *untrusted* certificate is available. The *keytool* application is available as part of the Java software development kit and can be used to generate a security certificate. A certificate is called untrusted when it is not signed by a trusted third party and, therefore, has not been verified. Running this tools is simple; doing so generates a new file called .keystore, which contains the security certificate.

```
>keytool -genkey -alias pjbank -keyalg RSA -keystore .keystore
Enter keystore password: dollars
What is your first and last name?
 [Unknown]: Robert Brunner
What is the name of your organizational unit?
 [Unknown]: Online Banking
What is the name of your organization?
 [Unknown]: Persistent Java Bank
What is the name of your City or Locality?
 [Unknown]: Anytown
What is the name of your State or Province?
 [Unknown]: Anystate
What is the two-letter country code for this unit?
 [Unknown]: US
Is CN=Robert Brunner, OU=Online Banking, O=Persistent Java Bank, L=Anytown,
ST=Anystate, C=US correct?
 [no]: yes

Enter key password for <pjbank>
        (RETURN if same as keystore password):
```

To simplify using this keystore with Tomcat, both passwords should be identical. The next step is to move the newly generated keystore file to a suitable location, such as the WEB-INF directory of the target Web application. Once this is done, Tomcat needs to be configured to first support Secure Socket Layer (SSL) connections and second, to locate and use the new untrusted certificate. Fortunately, this is rather simple because the information is already in the Tomcat's server.xml configuration file and merely needs to be uncommented (along with a minor edit). The server.xml file is located in the conf subdirectory of your Tomcat installation directory. After removing the comments and specifying the location of the keystore file, the relevant section of your server.xml file should be identical to the following example (you will need to be sure that the keystoreFile attribute is correctly set).

```
<!-- Define a SSL Coyote HTTP/1.1 Connector on port 8443 -->

<Connector className="org.apache.coyote.tomcat5.CoyoteConnector"
  port="8443" minProcessors="5" maxProcessors="75"
  enableLookups="true" disableUploadTimeout="true"
  acceptCount="100" debug="0" scheme="https" secure="true">
```

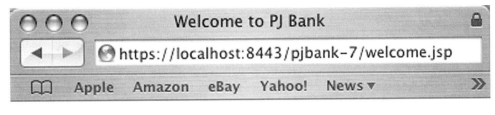

Figure 7.4: The welcome.jsp page, displayed using SSL.

```
<Factory className="org.apache.coyote.tomcat5.CoyoteServerSocketFactory"
 clientAuth="false" protocol="TLS"
 keystoreFile="webapps/pjbank-7/WEB-INF/.keystore" keystorePass="dollars"/>

</Connector>
```

To verify that everything is working, browse to *https://localhost:8443/pjbank-7/welcome.jsp*, which is shown in Figure 7.4. As you do so, you may receive a warning saying you are about to view information over a secure connection, which you can safely ignore. Combining the HTTPS connection with one of the three previously discussed authentication measures results in a secure and encrypted communication channel, suitable for most Web applications.

Exercises

1. Modify the controller Servlet presented earlier in this chapter to handle two cases: continue shopping or proceed to checkout.

2. Write a Servlet Filter that informs users that their shopping cart is empty and redirects them to the referring page.

3. Write a Servlet that calculates shipping costs, using an arbitrary algorithm. The Servlet should pass the shipping calculation to a presentation JSP page using an HTTP session attribute.

4. Write a JSP page that displays the contents of a shopping cart (which should be the ShoppingCartBean created in Chapter 3) and calculates the total price, including shipping costs calculated from the Servlet created in Exercise 3.

5. Write a new style sheet that works with the JSP page written for Exercise 4 to present its information in a more professional manner.

6. Using Form-based authentication and HTTPS, write a JSP page that accepts credit card information to complete a sale.

7. Write as many JavaScript functions as necessary to perform minimal client-side validation of the credit card form. For example, you should verify that a VISA card has 16 digits, that the expiration date is valid, and that the name and address fields are not empty.

appendix **A**

Tool Installation

All the tools used in this book are freely available online. In addition, the source code for the book, including all ancillary files, is also available online at *http://www.mkp.com/practical/jsp*. In general, Java 2, version 1.4.1 or higher, is assumed to be installed already. All code has been tested on machines running Microsoft Windows XP and Macintosh OSX.

A.1 Installing Tomcat

The Apache Jakarta Tomcat server provides the official reference implementation for the JavaServer Pages and Servlet specifications. As a result, if your Web application works with Tomcat, it is guaranteed to work with any other compliant server. Thus, the Tomcat server is a useful application, even if you are not planning to use it for production. In addition, at the time of this writing, only Tomcat supports the JSP 2.0 technology detailed herein.

The Tomcat server is available from the Apache Software Foundation, under the Jakarta project, at *http://jakarta.apache.org/tomcat*. The examples in this book require Tomcat version 5.0 or higher, which can be downloaded from the Jakarta Web Site, by selecting the binaries link, which is listed under downloads on the left-hand side of the main Jakarta Web page. Currently, the latest version is Tomcat 5.0.3 Alpha, but you should select the most recent version listed.

Tomcat can be installed anywhere; all paths are relative to the base installation directory. When necessary, it will be assumed that Tomcat is installed in C:\tomcat, but you should be able to easily transform this to your actual installation directory. To run Tomcat, execute either the startup.bat or startup.sh file, depending on whether you are

165

running a Windows machine or a Unix-based machine. These files are located in the bin subdirectory of your Tomcat installation directory. Proper shutdown of the Tomcat server requires running the shutdown.bat or shutdown.sh script. Depending on your operating system, Tomcat may require you to set the JAVA_HOME environment variable, which should point to the base Java installation directory.

A.2 Installing the Example Code

The example code is distributed on a per chapter basis as both a zip file and as a Web application archive (WAR) file from the book's Web page at *http://www.mkp.com/practical/jsp*. You only need one version of each Chapter's source code (in other words only the zip file or only the WAR file). If you download the zip file, it will need to be unzipped into the Web application deployment directory for the application server you are using. For the Tomcat server, this is the webapps directory. If you download the WAR file, it merely needs to be placed in the Web application deployment directory, which for Tomcat is the webapps directory. The application server will automatically expand the WAR file.

    The code for each chapter is collected into individual contexts, named pjbank-X, where X is replaced by the actual chapter number. Each context has an index page, called index.jsp, that allows for simple navigation to each sample JSP page demonstrated within the relevant chapter. To view the ancillary files, such as stylesheets, scripts, tag files, or Java source code files, you will need to traverse the directory structure and open the files of interest in a text editor.

A.3 Installing the JSP Standard Tag Library

The JSP Standard Tag Library (JSTL) is also available from the Jakarta project of the Apache Software Foundation. Once again, the official reference implementation for JSTL is freely available from the Jakarta Standard Taglib Web site at *http://jakarta.apache.org/ taglibs/doc/standard-doc/intro.html*. Jakarta actually hosts a number of tag libraries, which, while not part of the standard tag library, may prove useful to when building a Web application.

    To use the JSTL with either the book's sample code or your own Web application, simply download the JSTL and place the relevant JAR files in the lib subdirectory of your application's WEB-INF directory. If multiple Web applications require these JAR files, they should be placed in the server's common lib directory. For Tomcat, this is the common\lib subdirectory of your Tomcat installation. Currently, the simplest method to use the JSTL with the book's sample code is to simply copy all JAR files in the standard-1.0.3\lib directory, created when the JSTL download file is unzipped, to the Tomcat server's common lib directory.

A.4 Installing MySQL

Several examples in this book have required a database system. For simplicity, these examples have used the MySQL database, which is freely available from the MySQL Web site at *http://www.mysql.com*. MySQL also provides a free JDBC driver called Connector/J from their Web site. The examples in this text have been verified to work with MySQL database server version 4.0.13 and version 3.0.8 of the Connector/J JDBC driver. These examples can easily be converted to work with any other database that supports JDBC, including Microsoft SQL Server, Oracle, and DB2. Further details on using the example code with these other databases are provided in Chapter 5.

A.4.1 Installation

The database software installation is straightforward, with both Windows and Macintosh OSX installer packages, and Linux RPM packages available at the MySQL download site. On a Windows system, the simplest installation location is C:\mysql, although other directories are possible as well. On UNIX-based systems, the software can be installed in a system-wide location, such as /usr/local/mysql, or in a user's home directory. In either case, the option to run the database server as an operating system service is available, but it is not required for the examples in this book. On Unix-based systems, additional steps may be required before proceeding. The information detailing these steps can be found in documentation that is included with the MySQL product as part of the download and installation process.

To use MySQL and the Connector/J JDBC driver (or another database and JDBC driver) with your Web application, the JAR file containing the JDBC driver should be installed in the WEB-INF subdirectory of any Web application that requires a database connection. Alternatively, a JDBC driver can be shared across multiple Web applications by placing it in a shared location. For the Tomcat server, this is the common\lib subdirectory of the Tomcat installation. Before testing the examples, the Tomcat server will need to be restarted (if already running) to properly pick up the JDBC JAR file.

A.4.2 Creating the Database

For the database examples in this book to work, a database must be created and accessible. After downloading and installing the MySQL database, the first step is to start the database server. If this was not automatically done during installation, it can be easily done on Microsoft Windows systems by running the mysqld program, which is located in the bin subdirectory of your MySQL installation (for example, C:\mysql). For more information on the equivalent procedure for a Unix-based system, consult the online documentation.

The next step is to assign a password to the database's root user account. If you are using an existing MySQL installation, this step can be safely skipped. You will, however, need to have access to the MySQL root account or else have your database administrator perform the pjbank database creation step. Although there are several different methods to assign a password to the root account, the easiest is the mysqladmin tool, which is also located in the bin subdirectory of your MySQL installation. Executing the following command at a command prompt from within the bin directory, will assign the password dollars to the database root account.

```
mysqladmin -u root password dollars
```

The next step is to create the pjbank database and grant access privileges for this new database to a regular user, named jack. This new user account will be used from our JSP pages to access the pjbank database. This step must be done using the database root account. To simplify the process, the database.sql command file, which is available as part of the book's sample code, can be used with the mysql tool, which is located in the bin subdirectory of your MySQL installation.

The following example runs the mysql tool from a command prompt within the bin directory as the root user and executes the SQL commands in the database.sql file. You will need to provide the full path to the database.sql file, or else copy it to the bin subdirectory of your MySQL installation, prior to running this command. The root account password will need to be entered at the password prompt. If you get an ERROR 1045: Access denied for user: 'root@127.0.0.1' (Using password: YES) message, try running the command without the -p flag.

```
mysql -u root -p < database.sql
```

The commands in the database.sql file first delete the pjbank database, if it already exists. This allows you to easily recreate the initial setup. Next, the pjbank database is created. The final two commands grant access privileges to the user account named jack, which has a password jill. These two statements differ in that the first GRANT statement allows jack to connect to the pjbank database from any machine, while the last GRANT statement explicitly names the localhost machine. MySQL handles the localhost slightly differently than remote hosts, hence the need for both statements.

Example A.1 database.sql

```
DROP DATABASE IF EXISTS pjbank ;

CREATE DATABASE pjbank ;

GRANT ALL PRIVILEGES ON pjbank.* TO jack@"%"
IDENTIFIED BY 'jill' WITH GRANT OPTION ;

GRANT ALL PRIVILEGES ON pjbank.* TO jack@localhost
IDENTIFIED BY 'jill' WITH GRANT OPTION ;
```

The final step is to create the database table that holds the data used in the examples. The command to perform this is stored in the table.sql command file and can be used with the mysql tool, but this time it should be run from the jack database account. The following example runs the mysql tool from a command prompt within the bin directory as the jack user and executes the SQL commands in the table.sql file. As before, you will need to provide the full path to the table.sql file. The jack account password, which is jill, must be entered at the password prompt.

```
mysql -u jack -p pjbank < table.sql
```

The table.sql command file first deletes the portfolio table if it exists, which allows the table to be recreated. This is done using the DROP TABLE command. Next, the CREATE TABLE command is used to create a table named portfolio in the pjbank database to hold the data for the examples used in this book. The portfolio table has four columns: name, shares, pprice, and cprice.

Example A.2 table.sql

```
DROP TABLE IF EXISTS portfolio ;

CREATE TABLE portfolio (
name VARCHAR(20),
shares INT(6),
pprice DOUBLE(16,2),
cprice DOUBLE(16,2)) ;
```

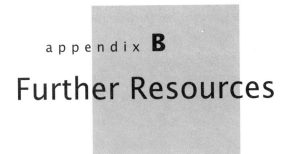

appendix **B**

Further Resources

This appendix contains further information on the topics introduced in this book. This information includes both online content as well as published material. No effort was made to be exhaustive; these lists are merely presented to help the interested reader find more information on the respective subjects.

B.1   The World Wide Web

The official home for all things related to the World Wide Web is the World Wide Web Consortium (W3C). The W3C homepage is at *http://www.w3.org*. The HTTP version 1.1 specification is available at *http://www.w3.org/Protocols/rfc2616/rfc2616.html*, and the HTML version 4.0 specification is available at *http://www.w3.org/TR/html4*.

Other useful specifications and their associated homepages include:

- Language codes: *http://www.oasis-open.org/cover/iso639a.html*
- Country codes: *http://www.iso.ch/iso/en/prods-services/popstds/countrynamecodes.html*
- Character encodings: *http://www.iana.org/assignments/character-sets*
- XPath: *http://www.w3.org/TR/xpath*

B.2   Java

The official homepage for all things Java is *http://java.sun.com*. This Web site includes a free, simple tutorial available at *http://java.sun.com/docs/books/tutorial*. The Java language has been divided into three editions. The Java technology used for building Web applications is part of the Java 2 Enterprise Edition (J2EE), which is detailed at *http://java.sun.com/j2ee*.

There are a number of good books that introduce the Java programming language, including the following (in no particular order).

- *Thinking in Java* by Bruce Eckel

- *Core Java* by Cay Horstmann and Gary Cornell

- *Java, Practical Guide for Programmers* by Zbigniew Sikora

- *Java Cookbook* by Ian Darwin

B.3   Java Servlets

Although this text provides only a cursory discussion of Java Servlets, considerably more details are available elsewhere. The official homepage for Servlet technology is *http://java.sun.com/products/servlet*. The complete, and final, place to look for the details on Servlet technology is the Servlet Specification, which can be accessed from the Servlet homepage. The API documents for the various Servlet classes, including HttpServletRequest, HttpServletResponse, and HttpSession, are available online at *http://java.sun.com/j2ee/1.4/docs/api/javax/servlet/http/package-summary.html*.

There are also a number of good books that present Servlet (in addition to JSP) technology in varying levels of sophistication, including the following.

- *Java Servlet Programming* by Jason Hunter

- *Core Servlets and JavaServer Pages* by Marty Hall

- *More Servlets and JavaServer Pages* by Marty Hall

- *CodeNotes for J2EE: EJB, JDBC, JSP, and Servlets* by Gregory Brill

B.4   JavaServer Pages

The official homepage for JavaServer Page technology is *http://java.sun.com/products/jsp*, which contains additional information, links to the official JSP specification, and online resources such as tutorials and articles.

In addition to the Java Servlet books listed previously, there are also a number of good JSP books, including the following.

- *JavaServer Pages* by Hans Bergsten

- *Advanced JavaServer Pages* by David Geary

B.5 The JSP Standard Tag Library

The JSTL specification is an incredibly readable standards document and is an excellent place to look for more information on the specifics of the different tags available within the JSTL. In particular, the following chapters present information on specific JSTL tags:

- Expression Language: Chapter 3
- Core Tags: Chapters 4, 5, 6, and 7
- Internationalization Tags: Chapter 8
- Formatting Tags: Chapter 9
- XML Tags: Chapters 11, 12, and 13
- SQL Tags: Chapter 10

This relatively new technology also has a number of books written about it, including the following.

- *Core JSTL* by David Geary
- *JSTL in Action* by Shawn Bayern
- *JSTL: Practical Guide for Java Programmers* by Sue Spielman

B.6 Databases and JDBC

A good site for more information is the official JDBC site at *http://java.sun.com/products/jdbc*. In addition, more information on SQL can be found at *http://www.sql.org*. A number of books provide more information on using JDBC to connect a Java application to a database, including the following.

- *Database Programming with JDBC and Java* by George Reese
- *JDBC: Practical Guide for Java Programmers* by Gregory Speegle
- *JDBC API Tutorial and Reference* by Maydene Fisher, et al.

Database-specific information, including the use of a JDBC driver, can be found at the databases' respective Web sites:

- MySQL: *http://www.mysql.com*
- Oracle: *http://www.oracle.com/ip/deploy/database/oracle9i*
- DB2: *http://www-3.ibm.com/software/data/db2*
- Microsoft SQL Server: *http://www.microsoft.com/sql*
- PostgresSQL: *http://www.postgresql.org*

B.7   Internationalization and Localization

The official documentation for internationalization using Java can be found at *http://java.sun.com/j2se/1.4.1/docs/guide/intl/index.html*. In addition, the online Java tutorial contains a gentle introduction to this subject at *http://java.sun.com/docs/books/tutorial/i18n*. The best book on this subject is *Java Internationalization* by David Czarnecki and Andy Deitsch.

B.8   Security

The official homepage for Java Security is *http://java.sun.com/security*. In addition, security with Web applications is discussed in Chapter 12 of the Servlet Specification. Many of the JSP and Servlet texts mentioned earlier detail security as well. The best book on this subject is *Java Security* by Scott Oaks.

B.9   Web Applications

The heading "Web applications" covers a lot of ground, some of which has been discussed within other sections in this appendix. Some of the remaining non-Java technologies include the following.

- Struts: *http://jakarta.apache.org/struts*

- Cascading Style Sheets: *http://www.w3.org/Style/CSS*

- ECMAScript: *http://www.ecma-international.org/publications/standards/ECMA-262. HTM*

Struts technology is eventually likely to be replaced by JavaServer Faces, which is detailed at *http://java.sun.com/j2ee/javaserverfaces*.

Index

THE MORGAN KAUFMANN SERIES
IN PRACTICAL GUIDES

JSTL: Practical Guide for JSP Programmers

Sue Spielman, Switchback Software, Conifer, CO
ISBN 0-12-656755-7 • 256 pages

*An invaluable reference for any JSP developer's library.
Sue makes the complicated seem simple with her
conversational writing style and well thought out examples
and analogies.*

> — Matt Houser, J2EE Developer with The Washington Post
> and former Sun Microsystems Java Instructor

JDBC: Practical Guide for Java Programmers

Gregory D. Speegle, Baylor University, Waco, TX
ISBN 1-55860-736-6 • 130 pages

This easy-to-use book consists of a focused project-oriented
tutorial for practitioners who want to learn JDBC quickly
and also have a quick reference to the API. Where other
books on the topic don't have an instructional component
or contain too much information outside the scope of JDBC,
this concise book provides just the essentials one needs to
know to get up-and-running with programming using JDBC.

Java: Practical Guide for Programmers

Michael Sikora , Independent Consultant, U.K.
ISBN 1-55860-909-1 • 150 pages

As commercial businesses move away from client server
systems to developing multi-tiered web-based systems,
programmers will find that learning Java will be a requirement for their skill sets. This is a perfect supplement for
anyone who need to get up-to-speed quickly on the basics
of Java programming and for those interested in switching
to Java.